LOVE, LIES, *and* MURDER *in* NORTHERN OHIO

LOVE, LIES, *and* MURDER *in* NORTHERN OHIO

Wendy Koile

Published by The History Press
An imprint of Arcadia Publishing
Charleston, SC
www.historypress.com

First published 2026

Manufactured in the United States

ISBN 9781467155892
Hardcover ISBN 9781540299703

Library of Congress Control Number applied for

Notice: The information in this book is true and complete to the best of our knowledge. It is offered without guarantee on the part of the author or The History Press. The author and The History Press disclaim all liability in connection with the use of this book.

To Matt, my husband, for your unending support and faith in me

CONTENTS

ACKNOWLEDGEMENTS

First, I would like to thank my commissioning editor, John Rodrigue, for his patience, support, and knowledge. I would also like to thank the entire team at The History Press for their expertise in all things book publishing.

Second, I would like to extend my appreciation for numerous librarians, curators, historians, and guardians of important artifacts for your assistance in my quest to track down stories and images. Your time and skills are invaluable to researchers and writers.

Next, a special thanks to my writing groups and friends, including The Brain Trust and my Zanesville group, Pam, Larissa, and Tracey. You have all been my support and cheerleaders, some of you for many years.

Additionally, I would like to express my love and appreciation for my best writing friend, Jane Ann Turzillo. You have been there through every project, always offering support and laughter to get me through it.

Lastly, and most importantly, I would like to thank my family, my inner circle! Your encouragement and belief in me means more than you can ever know.

INTRODUCTION

On September 22, 1921, forty-three-year-old Minne Derr of Akron snapped. After her husband, Alvin, arrived home late again and refused to give an explanation regarding his whereabouts that evening, the couple of six years quarreled bitterly before Alvin stormed off to bed. Seething, Minnie waited until Alvin was asleep and then proceeded to pour acid onto the father of her five children. Inhaling the fumes, Alvin Derr died within minutes of the attack.

Like the Derrs' tragic story, murders fueled by romantic motives often involve layers of passions and emotions that have reached a boiling point. These crimes leave investigators attempting to pinpoint a specific motive and the media, as well as its audience, devouring each newly discovered, often salacious crumb discovered along the way. With the case of Alvin and Minnie Derr, at the outset the murder seemed driven by a wife's unchecked emotion but was soon found to be one prompted by years of infidelity and deceit when it was discovered that Alvin had a longtime girlfriend on the side. Perhaps it is these discoveries, this revealing of intimate details, that make murders between lovers so fascinating, even if the crime occurred decades ago.

In my research, I attempted to find Ohio cases that centered on "love murders," as they are called, that were fueled by a several factors, including jealousy, sex, and control. These factors on their own may not have resulted in tragedy but, when compounded with other influences such as mental health issues, created the perfect storm or "murderous violence" as defined in *Psychology Today*. In the 2014 article "Why Do (Some) Men Murder the Wives They Love?" Aaron Ben-Zeév, PhD, asserted, "The murder should be understood as a phenomenon anchored in a certain constellation of factors that combine and create the 'conditions for murder.'…It is more accurate to consider the motive for murder in terms of conditions that are favorable for the development of murderous violence, rather than in terms of one central personality variable."

Interestingly, while most of the cases in this book occurred during the mid-1900s, the motives or murderous conditions described mirror those concerning murder between partners committed in recent years. While early Ohioans may have had what we consider old-fashioned expectations involving romantic relationships and marriage, their feelings were no less passionate than ones found nearly a century later when it comes to love. It was and still is the inability to regulate those intense feelings and desires, among other compounding factors, that often culminates in horrific tragedy.

The following chapters include several accounts of people who lost at love. And while the complicated dynamics of these relationships, the motivations for the crimes, and the outcome of their actions are presented, a more simplistic pattern can be found within the tales; each story begins with love (or the idea of it), includes lies, and ends with murder.

THE FARMER TAKES A LIFE
(MEDINA, 1950)

Thus ended the first act of the macabre play of lust, love, and bloodshed.
—Akron Beacon Journal, 1951

Max Amerman was used to getting what he wanted. And what he happened to want in the fall of 1950 was pretty Randi Mast, whether she liked the idea or not. The only obstacle, which he saw as more of a nuisance than anything, was that his beloved was a married woman. Fortunately, that little issue could be taken care of by way of a shotgun and someone willing to pull the trigger. As luck, or in his opinion a stroke of genius, would have it, he knew just the person for the job, and by week's end, Randi Mast would be in his arms.

Max's infatuation with Randi, which later grew into an obsession, began in the spring of 1947 when the newlywedded Harold and Randi Mast arrived in Medina, hoping to put down roots near Harold's parents. Harold, twenty-three, just fresh from the military where he had served in the Medical Corps, was looking for work when he approached Max with a proposition. The young veteran and his war bride, Randi, twenty-two, whom he had met in Norway during his service, were interested in renting the small house on the Amerman property and sharecropping the eighty-acre farm with Max. The location was ideal for the Masts, as it was located about four miles south of Medina on Route 3, not far from Harold's parents' home.

A romantic-themed postcard popular in the early 1900s. *Author's collection.*

As it were, Max had been charged with tending to the Amerman farm, which he stood to inherit from his ailing ninety-year-old grandmother. What his grandmother did not know, probably because she had lost most of her eyesight, was that Max had little interest in the family farm and instead chose to spend his time gallivanting around town in his flashy new car. When the Masts arrived on his doorstep, he was overjoyed with the prospect of offloading the farm and his responsibilities. More importantly, the arrangement would allow him to get acquainted with the voluptuous Randi, whom he could barely take his eyes off upon their meeting. With that notion, Max carelessly scribbled out the terms of the lease, which worked heavily in the Masts' favor.

Over the following months, Max became a frequent visitor at his tenants' home, easily winning over the respect of Harold, who was by all accounts a kind and gentle man. With the first line of business underway, Max set his sights on the real prize. During his many visits, Max used any opportunity to engage in conversation with Randi. When she remained reserved or perhaps uninterested in his attention, he simply ramped up his game. If she was not impressed by his charm and intellect, then maybe a little wining and dining would do the trick. And so, by Max's insistence and courtesy of his unending supply of money, often the trio was spotted cruising around town in Max's Oldsmobile, dining in nice restaurants, or catching the latest films in nearby Akron. Unfortunately for Max, just as he thought he was making some headway, the Masts announced that they were expecting a baby.

To Max, the arrival of baby Elsie Kay Mast in the spring of 1948 merely created a pause in his plans. While he waited for the upheaval over at the Masts' place to settle down, he temporarily entertained himself with a little side project. Although he continued to drop in on the Masts and feign some interest in the kid, most of his time was spent with his new pal Gerald "Jerry" Killinger.

In the summer of 1948, when fifteen-year-old Jerry started working on the Amerman farm, his adoration for twenty-five-year-old Max was obvious. Not only did the boy jump at every chance to spend time with Max, which included jaunts around town, he basically hung on Max's every word as well. Max, thriving on all of this, was happy to cultivate the relationship, lavishing the boy with praise and all the things that his money could afford. Besides, not only did the kid idolize Max, but he also was eager to please him. And when Max learned that Jerry had been in trouble with the law the year prior for petty theft and break-ins, he was more than happy to step in and act as a sort of mentor, being the upstanding man that he was.

As Max focused his attention on his new protégé, life at the Masts' house fell into a daily routine. Randi, who seemed to enjoy motherhood, kept close to home tending to the new baby and other household chores. Harold, determined to be successful at farming although he had no experience, worked tirelessly around the farm. When he learned that government-funded agricultural courses were offered two nights a week at a nearby school, he jumped at the chance to perfect his skills. Yet even as they settled into life as a little family, Randi often expressed that she missed her parents, who had remained overseas, the grief only worsening as little Elsie hit precious milestones that her parents would never witness. Even when their dear friend Max began to frequent the household again, it seemed that Randi became even more distant, which Harold attributed to her longing for her family.

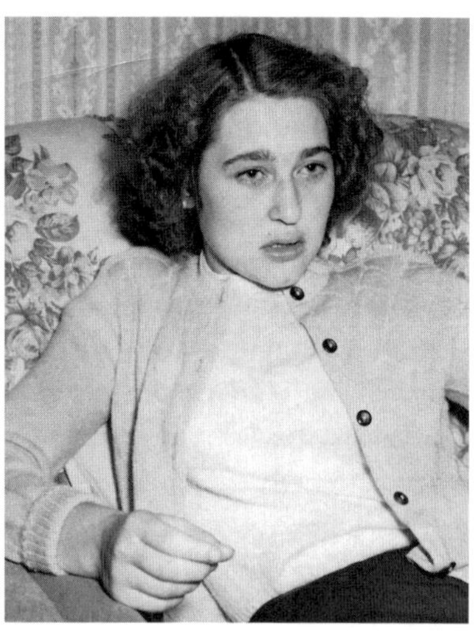

Randi Mast (1950), lover of Max Amerman, wife of Harold Mast. *From Acme Newspictures Inc.*

While Harold contemplated how to help his wife, Max, with Jerry in tow, once again became a constant fixture at the Mast home. Soon the visits turned into evenings out for the foursome, while Harold's parents looked after the baby. Not only did the group patronize establishments in Medina, but Max also insisted on treating his friends to trips to Cleveland, where they could experience fine dining and the best clubs in the city. Max's generosity, and his money, seemed limitless, especially after he officially inherited the farm when his grandmother died in 1950.

Around this time, perhaps seeing Max's openly flowing cash, Harold had an idea. After discussing the plan with Randi, Harold approached Max with a proposition, explaining that he needed $900 to bring Randi's parents to America. Max happily agreed to finance the loan, offering the cash with a 1 percent interest rate and repayment to be divided into small increments over a one-year period. As the two men shook hands, Harold had no idea that he, once again, was making a deal with the devil. The Masts were now monetarily indebted to Max, and he would attempt to use the financial agreement to get what he really wanted in return.

As arrangements were made for Randi's parents' arrival in the following weeks, Max continued to turn up at the Masts' place. Often, he would appear when Harold was tending the fields or at one of his agricultural courses. It was during these occasions that he began to make his feelings for Randi known to her. Although judging by her usual tense reaction to him, she was already aware of his intentions. When she failed to return his sentiments, he attempted to kiss her while she lay dozing on the couch one evening. As she struggled under his strength, Max explained that Harold had told him in confidence that he no longer loved or wanted his wife or child. With this, she ran crying from the room, slamming herself into an upstairs bedroom, but Max was not deterred. In fact, her rejection seemed to strengthen his resolve to have her. Consequently, his visits and open advances only intensified, often with Jerry standing lookout in case Harold returned early from his activities.

Eventually propelled partly by her discomfort and partially by her parents' arrival, Randi attempted to put a stop to the situation by reporting the unwanted attention to her husband. At first, Harold believed that there was some sort of miscommunication. After all, Max was such a friendly and giving person, perhaps Randi had misinterpreted Max's kindness as a romantic gesture. However, when he learned that Max had gone so far as to kiss Randi, he quickly changed his mind. Not one for confrontation, Harold decided the best course of action was to write a letter demanding that Max leave his wife alone. Both Harold and Randi signed the letter and assumed the problem was over, especially when Max discontinued his visits over the following weeks.

While the Masts believed Max was respectfully honoring their request, the reality was that his absence had nothing to do with respect. To him, this dismissal from the Masts' lives was the final straw. As far as he could tell, there was only one obstacle in his way, and that was the idiotic author of that nonsensical letter. Sure, he would stay away from Randi, but only because he needed some time to coordinate his plans, and what better place to do some thinking than on a lavish trip to the West Coast with his best buddy, Jerry. Thus, in the early spring of 1950, with the then seventeen-year-old Jerry all but dropping out of school, the pair hit the open road.

During their cross-country trip, Max reiterated his sadness over the Randi situation. Jerry, quite aware of Max's feelings for the lovely Randi, attempted to console his dearest friend. He agreed that the problem was not that Randi was not interested in Max—for how could that be possible—but the real issue was Harold's interference. Likewise, Jerry agreed that there was only one solution, and that was to eliminate Harold from the equation. And so, as the miles ticked by, the two joyfully proposed methods for doing just that. From bombing Harold's car to shooting him through his front window of the house, the ideas flowed like the Colorado River through the Grand Canyon, which they stopped to visit on their return trip.

By the time they reached the Ohio border, they had planned the impending murder of Harold Mast. First, according to Max, it was imperative that Jerry pull the trigger. Max would certainly do it himself, he explained to Jerry, but the fact was no one would suspect a teenager. Besides, he already had the perfect alibi planned for himself, which required him to be several states away at the time of the murder, so it was impossible for Max to commit the crime. Most importantly, if Jerry was willing to do this favor for his best friend, then Max would not only buy Jerry his own new car but also support Jerry financially for the rest of his life. With those rewards dangled in front of him, Jerry readily agreed to do the dirty work.

Next, they needed to secure the weapon, which they agreed should be a shotgun. This step took a little more in-depth thought, but luckily Max had another brilliant idea. Purchasing a gun from a local gun shop in late September, Max quickly went to work. To be certain that the 12-gauge shotgun could not be traced and to impress Jerry with his criminal expertise, Max filed the serial numbers off the weapon. Max then reported the gun stolen from his vehicle while it was parked in Cleveland. With the weapon now reported as stolen under an official police report, their confidence in their own cleverness soared.

Lastly, the pair decided that the timing of the murder was the most critical of all. Not only did they need to take out Harold without any chance of a witness, but they also needed a believable alibi for Max. Luckily, Max knew the perfect night for those two events to occur. Killing Harold undetected would be easy enough, especially when Harold arrived home late from his ongoing Thursday night agricultural classes. Jerry could simply hide in darkness and wait for the unsuspecting Harold. Once the deed was done, Jerry could slip through the fields completely undiscovered. As for Max, he would be sure to be seen near a different field, one where the New York Yankees and Philadelphia Phillies would play at the 1950 World Series.

With the plan finalized, Max and Jerry prepared for the big night. On Tuesday, October 2, Max left Ohio to attend the World Series on the East Coast, making sure to mention his plans to anyone within earshot. During his trip, he stopped at restaurants, purchased gas, and booked motel rooms.

At each stop, he was sure to introduce himself and chat with employees of those establishments and meticulously collect receipts at each stop. On Thursday afternoon, October 4, he cheered along with the crowd during Game 1 of the series as the Yankies beat the Phillies. However, whatever thrill he felt over the results of the game was no match for the joy of knowing what was about to happen in Ohio. As he checked himself into his hotel room in New Jersey, he pictured Randi, who would soon welcome his loving embrace.

Meanwhile, as Max fell into a restful sleep, nearly five hundred miles away, Jerry positioned himself just outside of view of the Mast home. Inside, he could see Randi and her parents sitting at the kitchen table, probably waiting for Harold to return before they all turned in for the night. Like clockwork, a little after 10:00 p.m., the headlights of Harold's car cut through the darkness as he turned into the driveway. Watching as Harold put the car in park, Jerry aimed the gun toward the driver's door. As Harold stepped out of the vehicle, Jerry squeezed the trigger and observed as Harold instantly fell to the ground. Assuming he had obliterated his target, Jerry dashed through the back fields, arriving at the borrowed vehicle that he had hidden just off the side of a dirt road a few miles away. While he maneuvered the car over the rural routes back toward his home, he listened to the wail of a siren cutting through the quiet countryside as emergency responders made their way to the Amerman farm.

By Friday morning, Jerry, like all the neighbors in the community, had learned that Harold Mast had died as a result of an ambush killing at his own home. If that was not enough of a shock, the police already had a plausible murder suspect with a strong motive thanks to information provided by Randi Mast and her family. According to deputies Otis Carlton and Steven Helli, who questioned the freshly widowed Randi, the couple's landlord, Max Amerman, was the culprit. Randi had explained how Amerman had made advances toward her over the past year and threatened "to take care of Harold." Randi's family, in particular her sister, corroborated Randi's claims, as she had witnessed Amerman's openly flirtatious remarks toward her sister while she had visited. Likewise, Randi's mother stated that Randi had often complained about Amerman. With this information, a manhunt was now in place for Max Amerman, who had not been seen since Tuesday afternoon, when he had supposedly departed from his cousin's home en route for Philadelphia to attend the World Series.

Over the weekend, as Harold's loved ones prepared for his funeral, Jerry attempted to call the Mast home to offer his condolences but was unable to get through the phone lines. On Saturday, not surprisingly, the police visited Jerry, still living at his parents' home, in an attempt to garner information about Amerman. Jerry explained that he had not talked to his boss and good friend for a few weeks, and the last he had heard, Amerman was headed to the big game to see his favorite team play. When the deputies questioned Jerry about his own whereabouts on the night of the murder, he explained that he had been on a date to the movies. Luckily, the policemen seemed to accept this information and continued their quest to locate Amerman—they did not have to search for long.

On Monday morning, just as Medina County Prosecutor William Batchelder Jr. and Sheriff Charles Williams were discussing the Mast case at police headquarters, in strolled none other than Max Amerman. Apparently, Max, on his arrival home late Sunday night, had learned that he was wanted for questioning in the brutal murder of Harold Mast. Displaying both sadness for the victim and confusion as to why he was sought as a suspect, Max explained that he had just heard the awful news when he returned from his trip. When he realized that the police were looking for him, he decided that he should turn himself in even though he had no inkling as to what happened to Mast, considering he had been hundreds of miles from the farm at the time of the murder. To prove it, he just happened to have World Series ticket stubs in his back pocket.

Although Amerman provided an alibi that was verified by a paper trail and a call to the Friendly Inn in New Jersey where he had checked in on Thursday night, both the prosecutor and the sheriff remained unconvinced of Amerman's ignorance and innocence regarding the crime. Even with his whereabouts confirmed, they could not let go of the suspected motive for the murder, which placed Amerman at the front and center of it all. When pressed, Amerman openly admitted his attraction to Randi Mast and his desire to marry her. Still, he argued, he would never kill the woman's husband as a means of winning her over. Besides this, as he implied to the detectives, a wealthy young bachelor such as himself would never stoop to such desperate measures to secure the love of a woman, as there would be no need to do so. Unimpressed and unconvinced, investigators decided to hold Amerman for further questioning.

Next, following a hunch that Amerman had not acted alone and learning of his unusually close friendship with teenaged Jerry Killinger, Prosecutor Batchelder and Detective Cowles brought the boy in for a more in-depth interrogation on Tuesday morning. After several hours of arguing his innocence as well as defending his dear friend Max, Jerry was strapped to a lie detector machine. After a few minutes of watching the polygraph needle swing wildly with each denial, Jerry showed the first signs of nervousness.

While the youngster sweated it out, the detective marched down the hall to where Max Amerman sat quietly, confident that he would be released any minute. Much to Amerman's surprise, Cowles announced that Killinger was singing like a bird in his makeshift cage down the hall. With this, Amerman dropped his head in defeat and stated that he was ready "to get it over with." Slowly, he detailed his infatuation and many advances toward Randi Mast, the cross-country trip where he and Killinger had planned the murder and the night that Killinger pulled the trigger while he secured his perfect alibi. He was also adamant that Randi Mast had nothing to do with her husband's murder.

Returning to the room where Killinger still sat hooked to the polygraph machine, the prosecutor easily secured a confession from the teen once Killinger learned that Amerman had told all. Surprisingly, the two confessions matched in all aspects, including the insistence that Randi did not help plan or had any knowledge of the murder plot, minus a few loudmouth-like threats from Amerman to deal with Harold. Additionally, Killinger provided his motive for the crime, stating that he did it for the car, the money, and to help his friend. As for the means to kill his victim, Killinger led investigators to a nearby dam where he had tossed the murder weapon.

After garnering the confessions and evidence from the killers, it seemed that it would be an open-and-shut case, but investigators knew that murder and subsequent trials usually unveiled layers of secrets and lies, especially when it came to love affairs. With this knowledge, detectives requested a follow-up interview with Randi Mast, who had been nearly bedridden since her husband's death. Whatever her involvement with Amerman had been, it could heavily influence the outcome of the impending trial.

With her doctor, parents, and sister by her side, Randi quietly reiterated her relationship with Amerman. Again, she explained that Max had made several advances both verbally and physically toward her, which she rejected. She also recounted the night that Amerman first tried to kiss her and how Harold had written a letter requesting that he no longer visit when Randi was home alone. Likewise, Randi's sister explained that Randi had complained about Amerman on several occasions. She explained that her sister was not only completely faithful to Harold but also unattracted to Max, who was overbearing.

As investigators continued to gather information, the Medina County judiciary system began preliminary proceedings concerning the two inmates housed in the county jail. First, and foremost, there was the question about whether seventeen-year-old Jerry Killinger should be tried as a juvenile or as an adult. If tried as a youth, he would complete his sentence in a detention center and most likely be released at age twenty-one. On the other hand, if tried as an adult, Killinger would face first-degree murder chargers with the death penalty on the table, the same as his counterpart, Max Amerman. After a thorough examination by Dr. John A. Hunter of the department of neuropsychiatry at Cleveland Clinic, who found Jerry sane and demonstrating high intelligence, Judge Derhammer ruled that Killinger would stand trial as an adult.

On October 12, Max Amerman was arraigned by a grand jury with a charge of first-degree murder in which he pleaded guilty. He was to be held without bond to await his trial, set for early November. Just over a week later, Amerman changed his plea to not guilty, which ensured he would have a jury trial instead of a three-judge hearing. Similarly, after learning that he would be charged as an adult, Jerry Killinger entered a plea of not guilty and accepted the offer from a Cleveland lawyer, Thomas Friel, to defend him pro bono. Trial dates were set for early November, with each man to be tried separately.

As the trial date neared, prosecution returned to the idea that Randi Mast was holding back information. To prosecutor Batchelder, her description of her relationship with Amerman did not add up. If she detested Amerman and his advances, why then did she continue to participate in the group outings for almost two years? Why would Amerman murder a man for a woman who supposedly denied his affection? Maybe it was time for Mrs. Mast to be treated to a more intense interrogation.

During questioning, Randi, still barely able to get out of bed due to her grief, explained the relationship between Amerman and herself once again to the investigators. Again, with her family by her side, she repeated that Max continually harassed her until she was forced to tell Harold, who wrote a letter demanding that Max stay away from his wife. Randi's sister and mother confirmed that Randi had frequently complained about Max. They both insisted that Randi was a devoted wife and she had no interest in Max, who "smoked and drank cup after cup of coffee." Additionally, Randi admitted that Max threatened to "take care" of Harold, but she had begged him not to hurt her husband, and believed the matter was settled. While the prosecution team was not completely sold on Randi's claim of innocence, they had little evidence to prove otherwise. That would change a few days later when they learned that someone was ready to talk.

Apparently, Jerry Killinger had a change of heart during his stint behind bars, especially when he learned what Amerman was up to from his own jail cell. His dear friend, the one who had promised to take care of Jerry financially, had deeded his farm (valued at $20,000), the $9,000 in his bank account, and his car to Randi Mast, all while the Killinger family desperately attempted to secure a lawyer with little means before accepting the offer from Thomas Friel to work pro bono. Not only was Max Amerman not going to support Jerry financially during the trial, but Jerry also would never receive the promised new car and hefty compensation if he ever got out of jail. As the realization that he had been played by Max sank in, Jerry decided it was time to share a few more details that he had previously left out of the story.

According to the dejected teen, the reported events leading up to the murder were partially true. Max pursued Randi, became obsessed with her, and planned the murder of Harold. What both Max and Jerry failed to mention in their initial confessions was that Randi had returned Max's affections. Sure, she would sometimes change her mind and attempt to back out of the relationship, especially once her parents arrived, but she willingly had been involved with Max both physically and emotionally. Jerry explained that he often was the lookout while Randi and Max spent some time in the dark corners of the barn. If the two could not slip away, they resorted to flirting right under Harold's nose, exchanging longing glances and tapping each other's legs under the table. Furthermore, when Jerry and Max went out West for several weeks, Randi sent Max numerous love letters.

With this new information, investigators called Randi downtown for another interview. This time, she, too, was strapped to a polygraph. Whether she was nervous because of the lie detector or perhaps she simply was ready to tell the truth, she admitted that she had thought she was in love with Max at one time. Eventually, though, she felt guilty and tried to end the relationship. It was at this point that Max began manipulating the situation by explaining that Harold did not love her and planned to leave her. When this did not do the trick, Max threatened that he would take care of Harold, in which case Randi begged him not to hurt her husband.

Finally, with a clearer picture of the relationship between the parties involved, both the prosecution and defense were ready for the first trial, scheduled for November 8, 1950, which would try Jerry Killinger for first-degree murder. Interestingly, a few days before the trial opened, the defense changed the plea from "not guilty" to "not guilty by reason of insanity." Throughout the hearings, the goal of the defense was to show that Killinger was weak-minded and had been manipulated by an older man. On the other hand, the prosecution attempted to prove that Killinger committed the crime for monetary and material gain.

Although the defense came in strong with a doctor's testimony stating that Killinger indeed suffered mental deficiencies, the prosecution offered a persuasive rebuttal that included testimony from Randi Mast herself, showing that the teenager knew exactly what he was doing. However, it was Killinger's own words that basically sealed his fate. During his time on the stand, not only did he confess to wanting the promised new car, money, and Amerman's approval, but he also demonstrated an obvious callousness toward the victim, stating that he thought Harold to be quite

The crowd waiting to attend the trial of Gerald "Jerry" Killinger, 1950. *From Acme Newspictures Inc.*

Gerald "Jerry" Killinger with defense lawyers as they prepare for his trial, 1950. *From Acme Newspictures Inc.*

stupid. More damningly, Killinger announced that he had waited in the dark for at least forty-five minutes for Harold to arrive home without ever giving thought to backing out of the plan. Summarizing this sentiment and moving the jury to tears, in his closing statements Prosecutor Batchelder stated that the murder of Harold Mast was "coldly planned for a year just as dispassionately as the killing of a chicken and a lot less dispassionately than some of us would kill a chicken."

After seven hours of extremely emotional deliberations, the jury returned with a decision. On the day before Jerry Killinger's eighteenth birthday, they returned the verdict of "guilty of first-degree murder" without recommendation of mercy. As the realization sank in, Jerry Killinger seemed to lose his footing and fell back into his chair. While his parents openly wept, the now convicted murderer was led from the courtroom with the death penalty looming before him.

If Killinger's trial was sensational and full of exciting debate, his counterpart's trial was anything but that. Instead, Amerman's trial, which opened in early January 1951, was basically a cut-and-dried affair. It seemed Amerman had accepted his defeat prior to the trial. During his hearing, the most excitement came when Amerman stated that Randi Mast was the "aggressor" in the love affair and she consistently wrote him childlike love letters expressing her desire to be with him, although no such letters had been found during searches of the Amerman property.

Nevertheless, Amerman insisted that it was this promise of her love that prompted the murder. In fact, he was so certain of her devotion that a few months prior to the crime, he had deeded his property to her in addition to taking out a life insurance policy naming Randi as the beneficiary in the event of his own death. Although his confessed motives were a delight to the media, the admittance did nothing to sway the jury, as he never once denied his guilt. On January 26, Amerman was found guilty of first-degree murder and would be subjected to death by the electric chair in November 1951.

In the meantime, the bereaved widow, still wearing black, set about selling the Amerman farm and collecting on Harold's life insurance. In the sale of the farm, valued at $20,000, Randi received roughly $3,300, and her four-year-old daughter was given approximately $9,600 to be distributed at $50 a month for her care until she turned eighteen, when she could draw on the remainder. An additional $6,400 was paid to Randi's lawyer. A few months later, in an insurance case, Randi was awarded $6,000 double indemnity for Harold's $3,000 policy, as she was found not to be an accessory to her husband's murder. And of course, there was still the promise of Max Amerman's life insurance benefits as his death date drew near.

Over the following cold winter months, both Killinger and Amerman served hard time behind bars at the Ohio Penitentiary in Columbus. Separated by only one cell between them, the convicts soon resumed their friendship. In an exclusive interview with a reporter from the *Akron Beacon Journal*, Jerry explained, "I was mad at Max for a while, but I'm not anymore. We are better buddies now than we were before. I can't be mad at Max. He has always been good to me. He has explained everything." In the same interview, Jerry explained how both men had experienced religious transformations and he was not afraid to die.

As their appointment with the electric chair approached, with Max scheduled for the chair on November 15 and Jerry on November 16, Harold Mast's parents sent a letter to Ohio Governor Lausche. In it, they asked that Jerry be spared the death penalty, as they not only forgave him but also fully believed that he was under the spell of the much older Max Amerman. Besides that, Jerry was a child at the time of the murder. Days later, a second letter arrived at the governor's office from Randi Mast, who insisted that both men should receive the death penalty for their crime and that no mercy should be offered.

Randi Mast and young daughter several months after Harold was killed, 1951. *From Acme Newspictures Inc.*

On November 15, 1951, Max Amerman was led to the chair, where he quietly accepted his fate and was put to death. On November 16, just hours before Jerry's appointment, his sentence was commuted to life in prison on the order of Governor Lausche.

By this time, Randi Mast, her daughter, and her parents had moved to New Jersey to escape the scrutiny and open judgment of the community. Unfortunately for her, Randi did not receive the benefits from Amerman's life insurance, as she learned he had rewritten his will two days prior to his death. In addition, she learned that Harold's parents were attempting to gain custody of Elsie, and they were asking that Randi's application for full citizenship be denied. After several months in court, the Masts failed in both pursuits, leaving Randi to begin a new life. Eventually, she remarried, and it is believed that she had additional children based on information in her sister's 2006 obituary.

In 1971, Jerry Killinger was released on parole at age thirty-nine. He went on to marry in 1973 and was known as a community-minded, hardworking man. In an interview granted with the same *Akron Beacon Journal* reporter he spoke with while on death row, Jerry stated on his parole release, "Sure, I took a man's life. He didn't deserve to die and I've paid for it. God how I've paid for it and always will." Jerry Killinger's earthly penitence ended at the age of seventy-three.

THE LOVER'S LANE MURDERS (LIMA, 1931)

These dark secluded spots, common to every community, are favorite parking places to maniacs and bushwackers…because they know petters make perfect prey.
—*The Daily News, 1931*

Every small town has a version of the story. The tale, a favorite among teenagers, centers on a couple that makes the most of a secluded local "parking" spot. The unsuspecting pair quickly learn of their grave mistake when a stranger, later identified as a sex-crazed maniac, begins to torment them. Depending on the version of the story, for one reason or another the vulnerable couple is unable to escape and their mutilated bodies are found the next day. Although the story is often told either as fun or as a cautionary tale to scare teenagers away from such nocturnal activities, the actuality is that many murders have occurred while couples were enjoying a night alone under the stars. Unfortunately for a young couple in Lima, Ohio, they became one of those real-life stories that makes truth more horrific than any creepy urban legend.

On the fateful evening of May 30, 1931, seventeen-year-old Thelma Woods and twenty-year-old Earl Truesdale were probably both a little nervous. After all, they had been introduced just the day before by Thelma's friend Bertha, and now they were preparing for their very first date. The plan was for Earl, who lived a few miles away in Elida, to pick up

Thelma at her home on North Jackson Street in Lima. They, like many of the local young people, were going to a dance held at McCullough's Park dance hall, which would celebrate not only the kickoff of summer but also the anticipated season opening of McCullough's Amusement Park that Memorial Day weekend.

Like clockwork, the well-mannered Earl showed up a little before 8:00 p.m. to meet Thelma's parents, and then the two headed off to the dance in his father's car. Earl, who had promised to take good care of the vehicle, was careful as they made their way to the park a few blocks away. While at the dance, the attractive pair seemed to be hitting it off, enjoying a night of dancing and socializing with their counterparts. At 11:00 p.m., the dance ended, but luckily for Thelma, her curfew was not until midnight, which left the couple an extra hour to cruise around town and extend the date just a little longer.

Meanwhile, as Thelma's curfew approached, Lois Woods kept herself awake to listen for her daughter's return. Fortunately, Thelma, even in her teenage years, was a responsible girl. Sure, her pretty daughter had her fair share of young men in constant pursuit, but Thelma always obeyed her parents' rules, especially when it came to dating. So, when her daughter failed to return home at her given curfew, Lois was instantly concerned.

Fretting throughout the night, both Lois and John tried to rationalize their daughter's absence. Perhaps the pair had car trouble or were involved in wreck, although the park was only about a five-minute drive from their home. Maybe they were just behaving like teenagers and Thelma was demonstrating her first sign of rebelliousness. Surely, she would be sneaking through that door at any minute. Yet by dawn, with no sign of Thelma or Earl, the Woods were panicked.

That same morning, in a residence about six miles from Lima, Earl's parents noted that their son had failed to return home as well. To the Truesdales, the parents of five young men, it was not unusual for one of their sons to stay out all night. In the case of Earl in particular, they would excuse the behavior, as the boy had been working from sunup to sundown since he graduated high school. Most likely, the Woods had put him up for the night to keep him off the roads so late. However, all these thoughts went to the wayside when they received a phone call from John Woods inquiring about Earl's whereabouts.

As the two families conversed, they all agreed that something was amiss. Running through all scenarios, the slim possibility that the two had eloped occurred to them. However, as they discussed this in detail, Don Truesdale

A postcard depicting McCullough's Park Pavilion where Thelma and Earl attended the dance. *Author's collection.*

FOR CLEAN FUN—VISIT

McCULLOUGH PARK

Opening Saturday, May 23rd

DANCING EVERY TUESDAY, THURSDAY AND SATURDAY EACH WEEK

EARL SITES AND HIS BAND—10 PIECES

GRAND OPENING DECORATION DAY, MAY 30

Big Display Daylight Fireworks

WE CATER TO PICNIC PARTIES
Free Tables
Clean Grounds
A SAFE PLACE FOR THE KIDDIES

THIS SEASON LIMA'S FAVORITE PLAYGROUND
Is Managed By
LOCAL BUSINESS MEN
EVERYTHING SOLD AT WHAT YOU HAVE TO PAY ELSEWHERE!
No Holdups *No Gyp Games*

BOATING
BATHING
DODGE 'EM
AEROPLANE SWING
For A Real Thrill
RIDE THE COASTER

An ad announcing the grand opening of McCullough's Park. *From the Lima Morning Star and Republic Gazette.*

stated that his son had only a few dollars on him. Plus, the boy had insisted that he would not become too serious with a girl until he could provide for her. Although Earl had worked at the locomotive plant in town after graduation, the Depression had caused the layoffs of many of those workers, with Earl being one of them. Therefore, Earl was working for mere cents on a local farm and had made no attempt to collect on recent wages. Likewise, Thelma had shown no interest in marriage anytime soon. Plus, she had not taken any money or clothing with her to the dance. To the parents, the idea of the two sneaking off to wed seemed farfetched.

Thelma Woods, who went missing after a Memorial Day dance in 1931. *From Acme Newspictures Inc.*

Continuing their quest to find the teens, Lois Woods contacted McCullough Park and learned from an employee that her daughter and Earl had attended the dance and stayed the entire time. Additionally, many of Thelma's friends reported that they had spent much of the evening talking and laughing with the now missing pair. Similarly, many dance-goers had noted Earl and Thelma drive off after the dance. One person also stated that they saw the pair driving near downtown sometime after 11:00 p.m.

By midday, with all possible explanations explained and associated contacts contacted, the parents had little choice but to call the police.

The county's newly elected sheriff, Jess Sarber, who had been in office for only a few months, answered the call. Sheriff Sarber's immediate theory was that the couple had simply run off, considering there was no trace of either since the previous night. This notion was short-lived, however, when later that afternoon, he received a call from the caretaker of the land near the abandoned quarry lake. Elmer Hubbard had found a deserted car matching the make and model of the one driven by Earl Truesdale near the near the edge of the water.

To Sheriff Sarber, it was apparent on arrival at the scene that something was off. First, the location where the car was found was remote and rarely traveled. There could be only one reason that the couple would have driven themselves to that spot. Being a lifelong local, the sheriff was well aware that youngsters often used the area as a trysting spot. Still, it was strange that the vehicle was left there if Thelma and Earl simply had been canoodling. Likewise, if the kids had had car trouble, they could easily walk

Earl Truesdale, who went missing after a Memorial Day dance in 1931. *From Acme Newspictures Inc.*

to town for help. Second, the car still had the headlights on, indicating that the car had been there since dark. On further inspection, the sheriff discovered that the key was missing from the ignition. Most alarming, though, was that there was no trace of the couple anywhere near the vehicle or in the vicinity of the quarry.

On Monday morning, Memorial Day, Don Truesdale arrived at the station and positively identified the vehicle that had been found deserted at the quarry. At the same time the police were questioning Don about his son and their family dynamics, they received another call from Elmer Hubbard, quarry caretaker. Sheepishly, Hubbard explained that he had found a blanket near the abandoned vehicle prior to the sheriff's arrival on scene the day before. Since the quarry was often used as a local dump, Hubbard thought that the blanket must have been discarded, so he had his wife wash it and they proceeded to use it for a baby blanket. According to Hubbard, after the police left, he remembered the item and decided that it could be connected to the situation at hand.

With this, Police Chief Kipker, now heavily involved, drove Don Truesdale out to the quarry to look at the item. Without hesitation, Don stated that the blanket belonged to the Truesdale family, and it had been in the car the last time he had seen it.

By Monday evening, with no word from the missing pair coupled with the findings at the quarry, it was now evident that the youngsters had not disappeared on their own accord. As the situation progressed from a simple search for two runaways to a full-blown missing persons case, County Investigator O.J Roush joined the Lima police in their efforts to search for the couple, starting at the most obvious place: the seventy-foot-deep quarry pond.

Over the next couple of days, a variety of methods were deployed to search the small lake thoroughly. First, as hundreds of onlookers gathered, a professional team from Toledo ignited sticks of dynamite underneath the water in hopes of pushing anything or anyone to the surface. As soon as one stick of the explosive was expended, searchers scanned the pond by boat, repeating the process six times. When this proved fruitless, volunteers—including the Spencerville National Guard (of which Earl served as a corporal), the William Paul Gallagher Post 96 of the American Legion, local volunteer fire departments, and local Boy Scouts—joined lawmen to begin the slow and daunting process of pumping the water out of the quarry.

Meanwhile, investigators continued in their mission to locate anyone with additional information connected to the disappearance. Specifically, with the case looking more and more like foul play, they were focused on identifying potential suspects, leading them to question one person with a possible motive and another person with an ideal opportunity to commit a crime.

First, James May, Thelma's ex-boyfriend, whom she had dated for three months during the fall of 1930, was hauled in for questioning. Perhaps the young man did not appreciate the fact that Thelma had started dating just a few months after her split with him. Maybe seeing Thelma and Earl at the dance, which he had attended, was the spark that led May to act on his jealousy, resulting in a crime against his ex-girlfriend and her new beau. Yet according to the young man, he had moved on, bringing his own date to the dance. As for his whereabouts after the event, he insisted that he had returned to his brother's home, where he played cards with some friends until late into the night.

With nothing to pin May other than a supposed passing romantic interest in the missing girl, authorities turned their sights to someone who had been involved in the situation from the start. Along with finding the vehicle, Elmer Hubbard had tampered, whether knowingly or not, with crucial evidence in a potential crime. More concerning though, not only did Hubbard have an opportunity to harm the couple at the secluded quarry, according to an anonymous tip, but he just might have had a perfect motive as well.

In an unsigned letter to the Lima Police Department a few days after the disappearance of Thelma and Earl, a local tipster explained that shady business often occurred at the abandoned quarry, also known as Lover's Lane. According to the writer, a sort of blackmailing racket was in full swing, especially when the weather turned nicer and brought daring teens to the ideal make-out spot. Once a couple parked and got to the business at hand, they were interrupted by a shadowy figure demanding their money and jewelry or else a call to the police or, worse yet, to the girl's parents would be made. Reportedly, Elmer Hubbard was the ringleader, as he had perfect surveillance and easy access to anyone dropping by the quarry for a late-night rendezvous. Thus, the quarry groundskeeper was brought into the station for a more in-depth interview, but he denied any knowledge of the blackmail or any involvement in the disappearance.

As investigators continued to look for clues, search efforts at the quarry were both slow and taxing. After ten days in, volunteers began to struggle with emotional and physical exhaustion. Similarly, many had donated their own equipment and taken time off work, which was taking a financial toll on their families. Compounding their frustration was the fact that they felt they had only minimal support from county officials when it came to monetary support, although later it would be shown that the county spent nearly $10,000 on the quarry search alone. Regardless of the brewing tension, both law officials and volunteers recognized they had only a day or two left to give in the search efforts at the quarry.

Finally, on the morning of day twelve, when the water level dropped to approximately thirteen feet, a female onlooker cried out as she spotted an object on a newly exposed ledge. Rushing to the area, volunteers blinked in shock and disbelief. There, as if delicately placed, was the bloated body of Thelma Woods, still clothed in her pretty red dancing dress. Quickly, she was covered up, just as the curious crowds clamored to that side of quarry to get a morbid look at the deceased.

If the police had any remaining questions about whether they were dealing with foul play, the recovery of Thelma's body confirmed that they were indeed investigating at least one homicide. On their first assessment of the body, they noted that the young woman's hands and feet had been tied with eleven feet of clothesline, and she was latched to a thirty-pound boulder. The fact that she was still fully clothed suggested that she had not been sexually assaulted, but it was nearly impossible to determine that aspect since she had been in the water for a prolonged period. Turning to the coroner for a more thorough exam, investigators learned that Thelma had been struck on the head with a blunt instrument, possibly a ball-peen hammer. Her cause of death was determined as drowning, as attested by the water in her lungs, which also illustrated that she had been alive when she was placed into the pond. Most assuredly, Thelma was murdered.

Based on the coroner's findings, investigators scrambled to find the weapon used to beat Thelma. Because they had not understood the gravity of the situation at the time the car had been found, police had not thoroughly searched the vehicle. Backtracking now, a few days after Thelma's funeral, two police officers appeared at the Truesdales' front door requesting to search the car. Within a few minutes, the detectives found an object of great interest to them. Shoved under the passenger seat was a ball-peen hammer with what appeared to be a spot of blood on the handle.

With the recovery of Thelma's body, the case spun in several directions. Since, so far, only Thelma had been found, the investigators speculated that something had gone awry between Thelma and Earl after the dance. It was possible that once the couple arrived at the quarry, Thelma might have rejected Earl's attempts at a sexual encounter. When he realized that she was not going to comply, he might have snapped, killing her in a fit of rage. Once he dumped the body, he could have hightailed it out of town.

The quarry, partially drained in the photograph, where authorities and volunteers searched for the bodies of Thelma and Earl while onlookers watched from above. *From Acme Newspictures Inc.*

Returning to the forefront, too, was the theory that James May was somehow involved. After all, they were now certain that a murder had occurred, and May had been in the vicinity the night of the killing. Making matters worse for May was the fact that this was not his first run-in with the law. Two years prior, he had been convicted on burglary charges, earning himself the moniker of the Pinochle Bandit, as he was known to burglarize local businesses and then turn up at the police station to watch officers in their nightly pinochle games. After he was found guilty, he was sent to Toledo to undergo psychiatric evaluation, at the request of his mother, but was found sane. Consequently, with his connection to Thelma and his criminal background, though not extensive, he was once again questioned, held a few days, and released when no confession or damning evidence was obtained.

As investigators struggled to pin down a suspect, a few relevant tips emerged. First, Pearle McCurdy, who lived at 924 West Kibby Street, about a block from the quarry, remembered that she had heard what sounded like an anguished scream between midnight and 1:00 a.m. on May 31 coming from the direction of the quarry. This offered a possible time frame in which the crime may have occurred. Next, another person residing on Kibby Street reported that they had spotted two figures lurking in their backyard the same night of the crime. Finally, D.U. Cummen, resident of 820 West Kibby Street, stated that a lengthy cord of clothesline had gone missing from his backyard around May 31, which could suggest that the crime had been premeditated.

At the quarry, now an official crime scene, efforts were redoubled, as it was probable that Earl would be found there as well. Working both day and night, crews used grappling hooks to search the bottom of the now shallow but murky water. Finally, on June 17, five days after finding Thelma and approximately 150 yards from where she was found, the body of Earl was located on a freshly exposed outcropping of rocks.

Like Thelma, Earl had been tied up with clothesline. Similarly, he had been weighted down with rocks in a makeshift bag secured to his trousers. The coroner assessed that he had sustained four blows to the back of the head with the same or a similar object used to hit Thelma. He, too, had been alive when he was dumped into the quarry and died as result of drowning. With his trousers attached, Earl's remains offered another clue when the key to the ignition was found in his front pocket. Most likely, Earl, careful with his father's car as he promised, placed the key in his pocket when the couple left the car and stretched out on a blanket together.

With both bodies recovered and the means of both murders determined, investigators were forced to look at the case in a new light. Originally, one of their main assumptions was that Thelma had been the target and was killed by her former jealous suitor or Earl had attacked her after his advances were rejected. Now working the case as a double homicide, they needed to focus on any possible motive someone would have to kill both victims. Yet even though they were attempting to investigate the case with fresh eyes, once again James May returned to the top of the list. On July 9, with undisclosed evidence and an affidavit signed by Don Truesdale against him, May was officially arrested. Fearing that locals might form a mob scene at the Lima Jail, Sheriff Sarber sent the young man to Toledo to be held until his arraignment hearing. In the meantime, both Sheriff Sarber and County Prosecutor E.M. Botkin had some questions for May, who was clearly agitated after being brought in again.

Grilling May about his alibi for the night of May 30 through the early hours of May 31, investigators were looking for any holes in his story. Over and over, May repeated how he attended the dance with a local girl and then called his father to drive them home. After dropping off his date around 11:30 p.m., May returned home. Always one for a good card game, May reported that he played cards with his brother Andrew until 2:00 a.m. Going on the tip that a scream was heard from the quarry between midnight and 1:00 a.m., Prosecutor Botkin homed in on the card game that supposedly took place at the same time the murders were believed to have occurred. Yet as hard as Botkin pushed May, the could-be killer kept to his story. Likewise, both May's father and brother corroborated his account of the night in question, leaving investigators with only circumstantial evidence at best. Once again, after three days of intense questioning, James May was released from custody with nothing to hold him.

Like May, another favorite suspect was brought back in for additional questioning. This time, police hauled in not only Elmer Hubbard but also his brother Fred. As with the arrest of May two days prior, investigators refused to disclose their reasoning behind it, but public speculation was that the two were ringleaders in the suspected blackmail racket at the quarry. Again, the police had nothing to prove the Hubbards' involvement, and the brothers were released after three days of interrogation.

Over the next several weeks, investigators continued to follow leads while the community mourned the loss of two innocent citizens. As weeks turned into months, locals began to lose faith that the case would ever be solved. The only hope was that the killer or killers would slip up and incriminate themselves somehow or that someone would have a heavy enough conscience to confess their sins. Fortunately, or so it seemed, in late January 1932, nearly eight months after the homicides, both factors were met when a prisoner at the Mansfield Reformatory was overheard discussing his involvement in the murders.

According to guardsman John Ward, he had listened in as inmate Lloyd Ziegler detailed the events of the quarry murders to his cellmate. Just a few days after the slayings, Ziegler, twenty, had been arrested for robbing a store in Lima and was sentenced to ten to twenty-five years of confinement, which was considered a harsh sentence at the time. With nothing but time on his hands or perhaps guilt in his heart, Ziegler felt the desire to tell the tale of what happened that fateful evening at the quarry just a few days before the robbery. When Ward overheard the conversation, he quickly reported it to Assistant Superintendent O.F. Garver, who then confronted Ziegler. Without hesitation, Ziegler wrote and signed a confession implicating himself and two others in the crime. Immediately, Garver placed a call to Sheriff Jess Sarber.

Within days of his confession, Ziegler was brought to Lima for further interrogation and his promise to point out crucial evidence at the quarry. Additionally, the investigators attempted to locate the two other suspects identified in Ziegler's confession: one Donald Smith and the second none other than one James May. Never too far from the law's radar, May was easily apprehended for questioning while Donald Smith proved to be more elusive. Although Ziegler stated that Smith was a Lima resident around twenty years old, neither the police nor locals could identify or locate him. Nevertheless, investigators were relieved to have possibly the biggest break in the case up to that date, and they had plenty of work to do in addition to rounding up the mysterious third party.

According to Ziegler's confession, the catalyst for the crime was May's jealousy over seeing Thelma and Earl at the dance together. After taking his date home around 10:00 p.m., a clearly intoxicated May returned to McCullough's Lake Park, where he watched Thelma and Earl together. When he attempted to talk to Thelma as she was leaving the event, she muttered a "hello" and explained that she had to go as Earl was taking her home. Openly agitated by this, May told Ziegler and Smith that they were going to follow the couple in his car. Trailing a few car lengths behind, the threesome watched as Earl turned down the road leading to the quarry. Leaving their car on Kibby Street, May, Ziegler, and Smith crept through the quarry area until they reached Earl's car.

As printed in full in the *Mansfield News Journal* on January 22, 1932, Ziegler wrote the following concerning the violent events that unfolded next:

> *We walked up to them. Jimmy said, "I thought we would catch you here." So him and Earl started to fight. Jimmy grabbed a hammer from the Truesdale car and hit the fellow and he* [fell] *to the ground. The girl screamed. Donald grabbed her and held her mouth shut.*
>
> *Then Jimmy said, "we* [might] *as well fix you too, old girl, so you can't say anything." So Jimmy hit her and she fell. I and Jimmy watched them until Donald went and got twine to tie them with. When Donald came back, we tied them up and Jimmy and I carried the girl over to the stone quarry and threw her in. Then Jimmy and Donald took Truesdale and threw him in just a little from where we threw the girl.*
>
> *Then we pushed the Truesdale car over a little by a trash pile and went back to the car and left.*

Finally, it seemed that the killers would be held accountable. Frustratingly though, within a couple of days, two events occurred that changed the direction of the investigation. First, when James May was quizzed about Ziegler's accusations, he claimed to know neither Ziegler nor Smith. When May was brought to Ziegler's holding cell, he protested that he had never seen Ziegler in his life. Although May's claim did not hold much weight by itself, the fact that Donald Smith didn't seem to exist offered May some credence. Second, and most damning to the new lead, Ziegler recanted his confession just before Prosecutor Botkin took it to the grand jury in hopes of obtaining murder indictments.

According to Ziegler, the reasoning for his confession followed by his swift retraction was twofold. Reported by the *Lima Morning Star*, Ziegler, during his recantation, exclaimed to the investigators that he would "rather be anywhere than in Mansfield Reformatory." Thus, with his disdain for his less-than-ideal accommodations at the prison and believing he had an unfair sentence for his previous crime, Ziegler hatched a plan to escape. Like many Lima residents, Ziegler was familiar with the details of the unsolved Lima murders as publicized in numerous newspapers and discussed within the community. Garnering specific details from the stories, Ziegler concocted a convincing confession sure to gain attention and, most imperative to his ploy, a trip to the Lima quarry. Once at the murder site, Ziegler planned to make his grand escape. Unfortunately for Ziegler, instead of heading to the quarry, his police escorts proceeded to take him straight to the Allen County Jail. On top of his failed escape plan, a couple nights in the county slammer convinced Ziegler that confessing to a murder might not be in his best interest. Apparently, his new jail mates taunted Ziegler that not only was he a "squealer," but he would most certainly "get the chair" as well. With this, Ziegler immediately changed his story and was hauled back to the Mansfield Reformatory.

Now extremely disappointed, investigators had no choice but to back off May and return to a crime with no suspects. To further add to the frustration, three days after Ziegler recanted, he once again attempted to confess to the murder, providing even more details that implicated himself, Smith, and May. Although Assistant Superintendent Garver was convinced that his prisoner was telling the truth, lead investigators refused to attempt an indictment without new evidence. Plus, to apprehend James May again would seem circus-like in the eyes of the locals, who were already losing faith that justice would be served.

Perhaps with the investigation seemingly going nowhere or maybe with discouragement over the Ziegler fiasco, the Woods family decided to hire Private Detective E.M. Baker from an agency in Lima in early March 1932. Working from the last possible lead, Baker made a visit to the Mansfield Reformatory nearly three months after Ziegler's first confession. Eager to talk, Ziegler told the detective that he had lied about the man named Donald Smith. Instead, the other culprit involved, along with himself and May, was a fellow inmate by the name of Bob White. Finding that Bob White did exist and was a resident of Lima before his stint in prison, Baker jumped at the chance to speak with White. Surprisingly, White confessed to his participation in the crime, opening yet another chapter in the investigation.

Lead investigators were swift to react to Baker's findings and resumed their own interrogations of both Ziegler and White. Although some holes in the two accounts existed and White downplaying his involvement, one factor remained the same between the new confession and the one from three months prior: James May. Therefore, in what was now becoming a routine, May was arrested and confined to await his fate for a fourth time.

Working quickly, investigators sought an indictment for the three, bringing in over twenty witnesses. In the meantime, White's story changed several times concerning his part the murders. Meanwhile, media focused on May, who proclaimed that he was a "victim of the vilest frame-up ever attempted in this state," as reported by the *Dayton Daily News*. As May declared his innocence and his frustration with the law, Bob White, in what seemed to be a pattern in the case, retracted his statement altogether, stating that he and Ziegler wanted a break from the confines of Mansfield Reformatory. By mid-March, May was freed, Ziegler and White returned to their detested prison cells, and investigators were back to a maddening beginning.

Approximately one year after the murders, an article in the *Lima Morning Star and Republic Gazette* titled "Year Old Probe Fails to Solve Pit Murder" stated, "The dual slaying has gone unsolved for a year and today apparently will go down in Lima police history as an unsolved crime." On the day of the one-year anniversary, a remembrance ad was placed in the same paper by the Woods family that read "In loving memory of our daughter Thelma Woods who met her fate at the hands of some unknown fiend on Decoration Day night May 30, 1931." The memorial was followed by a poem expressing their grief over their loss of their daughter. Both pieces illustrated the heartbreak and the hopelessness of the family and

Thelma Woods's parents awaiting the trial of their daughter's suspected killer. *From Acme Newspictures Inc.*

community as they faced a summer marked by horrific milestones while the "unknown fiend" went free.

As the weeks turned into months, it seemed that the media's prediction was accurate. Perhaps this would be one of only a few unsolved crimes in Allen County history. Maybe the killer was a stranger passing through who stumbled on an opportunity to carry out a morbid fantasy and then quietly escaped through the darkness that very night. If that scenario was correct, the murders would be nearly impossible to solve. On the other hand, if a local was connected, he or she either had been cleared or was staying one step ahead of the law. Either way, law officials were not giving up just yet, and their persistence was about to pay off.

In a shocking turn of events, in early September 1932, twenty-three-year-old Loren Truesdale, Earl's older brother, confessed to the murders during an interview with Orlo Weaver, a detective from the National Detective Bureau, who was hired by Prosecutor Botkin to reexamine the case. During the interrogation, Loren admitted to the slayings and said that his actions were prompted by jealousy and revenge. Loren, in the presence of his parents and detectives, stated, "Earl was always stealing my girls," and he was "getting even," as both men had had a romantic interest in Thelma. When Loren spotted his "kid brother" at the dance with the pretty brunette, his rage was sparked, and he proceeded to follow the couple out to the quarry afterward. There, he killed Earl in an act of revenge and murdered Thelma to keep her quiet.

While news spread across a shell-shocked town, Loren was sent to the county jail to await further questioning. Not surprisingly, by dawn the following day, in what was now par for the course in the case, Loren recanted his confession. He claimed that he was basically forced to confess after six hours of exhaustive grilling by Orlo Weaver, Sheriff Sarber, and Prosecutor Botkin. However, unlike the other confessors who withdrew their statements and were released, Loren remained behind bars as investigators clamored to take the case before a grand jury. A month later, Loren was indicted for two counts of first-degree murder, and a trial was scheduled for December. Prosecution declared that they would ask for the death penalty.

As both sides prepared for the trial, the public became divided. While many thought Loren was a perfect suspect who had yet to produce an alibi, many wondered if the investigators were attempting to close the case to appease the community and pinning it on Loren was an easy solution to a mystery that would otherwise go unsolved. Regardless of public opinion, it seemed the trial outcome could go either way as both sides scrambled to strengthen their arguments for or against Loren's involvement.

On the day of the trial, only one hundred were admitted into the courtroom, including two reporters from the *Lima Star*. Attendees watched as a seemingly emotionless Loren was brought into the courtroom. In an interesting turn in the case, as the prosecution rapidly fired questions at the defendant, the entire courtroom noticed that Loren had difficulty hearing the questions and frequently gave answers that did not make sense. Perhaps his emotionless gaze was not due to lack of remorse but due to confusion. Loren's obvious disability gave more credence to the defense's argument that his confession had been coerced. More damning still to the prosecution was that their key piece of evidence, a drop of blood on the hammer, could not be identified as either human or animal. On the other hand, the defense could not produce a witness to secure Loren's alibi, which stated that his car had broken down and he slept in it until five o'clock on the morning of the murders.

Finally, after ten days of trial, the case was turned over to the jury to decide. Following two days of deliberation, they were unsuccessful in establishing a verdict and reported a deadlock. A new trial was set by an obviously frustrated judge for January 30, 1933. In the interim, Loren was to be kept in the county jail to await his retrial.

Before the retrial, both sides agreed that Loren's sanity was in question. The prosecution would now seek to have Loren committed to the Lima State Hospital for the Criminally Insane instead of the death penalty. The defense claimed that Loren might not be fit for trial at all. In any case, Loren was tested by an outside organization that concluded that he was sane but had a hearing disability. A retrial was rescheduled for March of that year.

Unlike the first trial, though, the jury was quick to decide in the retrial. After just a few hours of deliberation, they declared Loren not guilty, and he was released on March 31, 1933.

Heartbreakingly, for the families, justice for Thelma and Earl did not and has not prevailed to this day. After the series of confessions and recantations, arrests and rearrests, and the Loren Truesdale debacle, both law officials and the families were exhausted and discouraged. On top of that, just five months after Loren's trial, Lima was once again in the national news as a new guest, John Dillinger, arrived at the Lima Jail to await his trial for a bank robbery. A month later, he was sprung free by a gang of colleagues who killed Sheriff Sarber in the process.

As the years passed, occasional reminders of the Lover's Lane Murders appeared in the local papers, memorializing the senseless tragedy. As those years turned to decades and then a century, the murders of Thelma and Earl became blended into the many layers of a well-known urban legend: the one that starts with a young couple parked on the outskirts of a small town unaware of the danger that lurks within the darkness.

THE TRAVELING MURDER SHOW (CAREY, 1933)

Sheriff Weatherholtz noted the bus parked along US Highway 23, just south of Carey, while en route to a local farmstead around 8:00 p.m. on October 13, 1933. While the sizable, unlit vehicle presented a danger to other drivers, he would have to handle the situation after he hopefully apprehended the elusive chicken thieves that had been working the area over the past few weeks. At 9:30 p.m., on his return trip, with no poultry snatchers in hand, he was surprised to see the Studebaker in the same precarious spot. Thankfully, though, when he rapped on the door, the female occupant quickly agreed to turn on her lights and stated that she would be on her way. Relieved that this was just another routine traffic check, the sheriff pulled back onto the highway and looked forward to the end of shift. He had no idea that several hours later, he would be called back to this exact location in response to a report of a dead body found in the neighboring field.

A couple months prior to the traffic warning and the little issue with the corpse, the parties responsible for the bus had started out on a lucrative business endeavor. In August 1933, by chance, or so it seemed at the time, an attractive woman named Eva Timmer had approached Robert Brown at his home in Powhaten Point, Ohio, and inquired about his Native American relic collection. She explained that she was in town with the Lacy Smith Show, a traveling carnival, and had learned of his amazing artifacts from the locals of the town where the show had been stationed for several days. As the two conversed, Robert explained that a carnival

A romantic-themed postcard popular in the early 1900s. *Author's collection.*

official had been to his home just the day before to buy his collection, which he declined to sell. When Eva pressed for his reasoning, he explained that after retiring as deputy marshal of Powhatan Point several years ago, losing his wife in a freak accident in 1928, and watching his four children leave the nest, now at age fifty-five, collecting was one of the few activities he had to occupy his time. Besides, he was proud of his collection, which consisted of thousands of extremely rare pieces that he had amassed over several decades.

As Eva quietly listened, she agreed that the relics and his time were precious—so precious, in fact, that he should consider sharing the collection with a wider audience by taking his show on the road. Lucky for Robert, Eva was debating leaving the carnival and hoping to start her own show. With her experience as a traveling performer, which included work with prestigious Pantages theaters circuits out west, she could assist Robert in the business as well as attract a crowd by playing the organ and reading palms. Additionally, Eva, forty-two, had also lost a spouse and could relate to his boredom and loneliness. Persuaded by her knowledge, sympathy, and charm, Robert agreed to the proposition just as the local carnival was pulling up stakes.

A few days later, after Robert purchased the Studebaker bus at Eva's suggestion, the two hit the open road. Immediately, Doc Brown's Indian Relic and Medicine Show became a successful barnstorming tour along the Ohio River region. Like most medicine shows that traveled with a focus on rural areas of the Midwest, Doc Brown's show offered a variety of amusements and curiosities. First, the locals were lured to the show by the exceptional musical talents of Eva on her organ. Once the audience was gathered, Doc Brown asked for a small admittance fee to see and learn about his extraordinarily large collection of Indian relics. The artifacts were artfully displayed in the front compartment of a bus, creating a unique traveling museum experience. To add to the mystical flavor of the show, Eva would read palms in the rear of the vehicle, predicting the future of anyone willing to pay a couple of dimes for the information. And thanks to her exotic looks due to her Middle Eastern heritage, many happily forked over their hard-earned money to learn what the mysterious seer could see. As the final piece, the pair suggested several healing remedies, available for purchase, based on Doc Brown's extensive knowledge of all things Native American. All in all, the show was a hit, just as Eva, in all her psychic abilities, had predicted. Consequently, in late September as the carnival and county fair season ended, Robert happily agreed with Eva to transition the show into a mobile museum with a focus on rural school districts as stops on their fall schedule.

As the fall tour got underway, the newly transitioned show became just as popular with the local schools as the medicine show had with the tiny villages along the river. With their educational show perfected, Robert and Eva decided to travel north in hopes of visiting untapped and more populous regions of the state. With one last stop at the elementary school in Lowell, Ohio, on October 12, the Doc Brown traveling show was seen leaving town late that same night to begin its northward trek. As the bus rumbled through the quiet streets, no one could have guessed that among the relics and camping gear lay Doc Brown, barely clinging to life.

Two days later, over two hundred miles away, just as Sheriff Weatherholtz arrived for his morning shift, two local men barged through the station's front door. Obviously distraught, the young men stated that they had noticed a pile of what appeared to be bedding along the roadside. On closer inspection, they were startled to see a human foot protruding from

A crowd gathered to attend a medicine show in rural Tennessee that targeted small farming communities, 1935. *Library of Congress.*

A postcard of Lowell, Ohio, where Doc Brown presented his collection for the last time. *Author's collection.*

the pile of pillows and blankets. When they described the location of their gruesome discovery, the sheriff immediately realized they were referring to the area where the bus had been parked just last night.

Racing to the scene, the sheriff and Deputy Paul Frey easily located the pile of pillows among the brambles and dried wheat stalks. As they removed the bedding, they found a deceased man, clad in only underwear. Examining the body, they spotted an obvious gunshot wound to his left brow, indicating they were looking at a possible murder victim. As the sheriff glanced along the roadside, he reconsidered what he thought had been a basic traffic nuisance the night before. Although the female occupant of the vehicle had not acted suspiciously, it did seem odd that she had been parked there in the first place. Now, he was certain that the bus, the woman, and the body were somehow all connected.

After the coroner and additional backup arrived on the scene, both Sheriff Weatherholtz and Deputy Frey anxiously began their pursuit in search of the bus. Acting on a hunch that the driver continued north on the well-traveled Highway 23, they raced along that path. Within hours, just outside of Maumee, about fifty miles from the crime scene in Carey, they spotted the large vehicle parked along the roadside. Seeing no driver in the front, they banged on the side compartment door, where the same woman, looking somewhat surprised to see the sheriff, answered the door. When they explained that she needed to return to Wyandot County with them for questioning, she put up no resistance, but she did insist that the large dog sleeping in the back needed to go along as well.

Back at the station, the woman, who they learned was Eva Timmer of Ferndale, Michigan, calmly explained that she had killed the man, Robert Brown, but she had done so for a good reason. According to Eva, Brown had made sexual advances toward her while they camped in the bus near the Marietta area on October 12. When Brown, who usually slept outside the bus, entered the compartment in the back where Eva slept, he made his intentions known. After fighting him off repeatedly, she reached for the gun that the two carried for protection against burglars. With no other choice, she shot Brown in the head to protect herself. After she realized that she had killed him, she was uncertain what to do with his body, so she continued north as planned. At some point, she decided that she wanted nothing more than to return to Ferndale, where her seven-year-old daughter was living with Eva's aunt and uncle. On her drive, she realized she could not arrive with a body in stow. Therefore, when she found a desolate spot along the highway, she dragged the unwanted cargo from the bus and deposited it there where, according to Eva, Brown's pet dog pulled pillows from the bed and placed them over his master's body.

While Eva and the dog were held in a cell in Upper Sandusky, a question of jurisdiction arose. According to Eva, she had shot Brown somewhere in southern Ohio, which would mean the crime was not committed in Wyandot County. Soon, the question regarding the location of the murder was answered once Coroner Schutz provided his findings. During his examination of the body, Schutz determined that Brown had been struck in the head hours prior to his death. He also sustained several injuries to his arms and left leg, and he had succumbed to the gunshot to the brow, which entered his brain. Most revealing, though, the coroner determined that Brown had died only hours before his body was found and processed, which meant he was shot not long before his body was dumped in Wyandot County.

Along with the physical logistics of the crime, the coroner's report exposed several issues with Eva's confession. On requestioning, Eva insisted that she had never struck the victim but had shot him before leaving Marietta. She also added that Robert had verbally threatened her by stating that he had killed two men in his life and would not hesitate to kill someone again if need be. She insisted that he had made several attempts to have his way with her, although she had no defense marks on her body. In this second round of questioning, she stated that the dog attempted to pull Brown away from her, implying that even the animal sensed the danger. Her only defense was to shoot her alleged attacker. It was obvious to the investigators that certain explanations were not matching the forensics involved.

As Eva elaborated and continued to add somewhat odd details to the story, both the coroner and the police were suspicious that she was holding back crucial details. They were now convinced that Eva had struck Robert in the head, rendering him unconscious with a flatiron that they found near the bedding compartment. Most likely, when Brown regained consciousness several hours later near Carey, she turned the gun on him and proceeded to discard the body along the roadside. Although investigators now had a clearer picture of the events leading to the murder, they were still uncertain about the motive. Fortunately, for this clarification, they did not have to wait long.

When Robert Brown's family arrived from Powhatan Point to claim his body, they quickly asserted that his wallet as well as important documents

The Studebaker bus that Timmer and Brown used to conduct their medicine shows, 1933. Later, the bus became a murder crime scene. *From Acme Newspictures Inc.*

A postcard of Lima State Hospital for the Criminally Insane where Eva Timmer was sent from Marysville Reformatory to continue her sentence. *Author's collection.*

concerning his artifact collection were missing. Without hesitation, the family indicated that they believed Eva took the items and that she had been planning to rob Robert of his collection, valued at nearly $8,000, and the recently purchased bus. They insisted that this had been her plan from the day she arrived on Robert's doorstep to the time she encouraged him to travel farther from his home, and the watchful eye of his family, over the past few weeks.

Based on the coroner's findings, evidence taken from the bus, statements from the Brown family, and Eva's inconsistent confession, Eva was indicted for first-degree murder and held under a $10,000 bond at Upper Sandusky.

On February 8, 1934, acting in her own defense, Eva took the stand in front on an overflowing courtroom, including her sister and seven-year-old daughter, and reiterated the details of the night Robert Brown attacked her and how she shot him in self-defense. Unfortunately, the prosecution was fully stocked with a variety of witnesses that easily poked massive holes in her testimony. From Coroner Stutz, who graphically explained his findings during the autopsy, to Shirley Smith, a ticket seller for one of Brown's shows, who stated that Robert and Eva shared the bed in the bus, witness testimony was extremely damning. As a result, after five hours of deliberations, the jury returned with a verdict of manslaughter, for which Eva was sentenced to one to twenty years, to be served in the Ohio Reformatory for Women in Marysville, Ohio.

Eventually, perhaps with her years of observing circus acts or maybe via her own mystical powers, in 1940 Eva Timmer escaped from the Lima State Hospital, where she had been transported the year prior. She was never apprehended. Authorities believed she most likely returned to traveling with carnivals and circuses.

OFF TO THE RACES (GREENVILLE, 1922)

The sixty-seventh annual Great Darke County Fair, held on August 22–25, 1922, in Greenville, Ohio, was on track to be one of the county's most successful fairs to date. With newly improved facilities, a pleasant weather forecast, and registrations for exceptionally fast racehorses, fair officials anticipated record-breaking crowds with attendees arriving from both Ohio and Indiana, as the county sits along the state border. What no one could have predicted was that one fairgoer was not there to enjoy a candy apple or cheer for her favorite horse. Instead, she was there to "do stuff," which entailed blowing away her husband's lover with a revolver.

For months, thirty-five-year-old Reba Fenwick of Muncie, Indiana, had been aware of the affair between her estranged husband, Vonnie Fenwick, and the married Mildred Foreman. Separated from Vonnie for the past year, she was not at all surprised, nor did she particularly care if he had moved on. What she did mind, however, was the fact that Mildred Foreman was prone to flaunting the relationship for the world and, most specifically, for Reba to see. According to Reba, Mildred had an infuriating habit of calling Reba to announce that she and Vonnie would be out and about on yet another exciting date. As Reba later told the police, "She has been calling me up and telling me she has been taking Vonnie around with her….She asked me when I was going to divorce him so that she could have him."

Over the course of several weeks, the phone calls continued, with each more taunting in tone than the last. Allegedly, in one instance, Mildred

A romantic-themed postcard popular in the early 1900s. *Author's collection.*

announced that she was picking up Vonnie so the pair could drive around in her car, and she wanted to know what Reba was going to do about it. Reba, clearly agitated by the question, responded, "I will do plenty about it." Reba also claimed that Mildred was more than happy to tell how "Vonnie ardently made love to her," as reported in the *Daily News Tribune*. As a result, with each communication, Reba's irritation and resentment grew, which was most likely the intention of the caller all along.

Eventually, on a hot Wednesday afternoon in August, Reba received a call that put her over the edge. This call was somewhat different than the rest; the caller was not Mildred but rather someone Mildred had asked to contact Reba. According to Reba, the unknown caller stated that Mildred wanted Reba to know that Mildred and Vonnie would be attending the fair to watch the races in Greenville, Ohio, the following day, and Reba could "catch them if she could." With this final call, Reba intended to more than just catch them.

On Thursday, August 24, Reba purchased a revolver and ordered a taxi to transport her to Greenville, an hour's drive from Muncie. Arriving at the fairgrounds around 2:00 p.m., she bought her admittance ticket, pushed her way through giddy fairgoers, and headed toward the grandstand. Watching from an inconspicuous area, she scanned the throng of nearly two thousand spectators until she spotted her target seated about midway up the bleachers. Without fanfare, she marched up the freshly painted steps, pulled out the revolver, and took aim at Mildred Foreman.

As the crowd roared and cheered on the horses, Reba, standing about fifteen feet from Mildred and Vonnie, fired the gun. As the bullet zinged through Mildred's leg, she screamed out in pain. Realizing she had been shot, she began to run down the grandstand. Reba, seeing Mildred bolt from her seat, fired off another shot as her target moved downward through the crowd. This time, the bullet hit the floor, ricocheted, and hit eleven-year-old Sarah Eyer in the leg.

While the crowd attempted to make sense of the scene, slowly working itself into a frenzy, Reba casually made her way back down the grandstand, noticing people gathered around Mildred, who had fainted on her descent. Whether Reba intended to shoot again is unknown, as the race attendees began to push and shove in effort to exit the stands. Miraculously, in the near stampede, Darke County Sheriff's Deputy Budd Corwin was able to apprehend the suspected shooter with little effort.

An ad for the 1922 Darke County Fair. *From the Richmond Palladium & Sun Telegram.*

A postcard depicting the newly built grandstand and racetrack in Greenville, Ohio, where Fenwick gunned down her tormenter. *Author's collection.*

While under police interview, Reba, seeming almost bored with the conversation, explained her motive for the shooting. She told police and later a reporter from the *Muncie Evening Press* "that she [Mildred] was welcome to get any man of mine away from me if she could, but I simply would not stand for her tormenting me about it." She also informed the police that Mildred had been her only target, and she placed no blame on Vonnie and had meant no harm to him. She was sorry, though, for the accidental shooting of the little girl. The following day, Reba was released to await arraignment and returned to Muncie with Vonnie accompanying her on the ride and then into her residence.

In the meantime, both victims made a full recovery and returned home. Although both sustained only surface wounds, Reba was in no way excused from her crimes. In fact, the more Reba talked to reporters, the more the public demanded that she pay for what she did, especially when she did not express any regret for injuring her rival. She also insinuated that she would not be harshly punished, as nobody had actually died in this case. And when she confidently pleaded "not guilty" in her arraignment, the Darke County prosecutor was determined to see that justice in his county was served.

As investigators dug into the case, they quickly realized that the Fenwicks, specifically Vonnie, were no strangers to the law. Over the past decade, he had been involved in the operation of an illegal gambling house, running a speakeasy, fist fighting, and public intoxication. In the months leading up to his separation from Reba, she had called the police on him on three separate occasions: once for drunkenness, once for physical assault, and once for spousal abandonment. Interestingly, they learned that the Fenwicks and Foremens had been friends for years prior to the incident. Even with Vonnie's full rap sheet and past relationship with the Foremans, investigators could find no proof that he was involved in the shooting, although they believed he knew of the tension between his estranged wife and Mildred. Nevertheless, they were certain that Reba had acted alone in her crime.

On February 27, 1923, Darke County Courts charged Reba with shooting with intent to kill. She was sentenced to an indeterminate period of imprisonment to be served in the Ohio Reformatory for Women. Yet surprisingly, she never spent a day in jail, proving her theory that she would not be held accountable for the shootings. Through a series of trials and mistrials that finally reached the Ohio Supreme Court and eventually the U.S. Supreme Court, she escaped her punishment time and time again as the courts failed to bring her to justice.

In 1923, Reba divorced Vonnie, who went on to have encounters with the law for selling alcohol during Prohibition. It is unclear whether Mildred and Henry Foreman remained married, although they were together for several months after the shooting. Apparently, Henry and Vonnie continued their friendship regardless of the alleged affair, as Henry was charged along with Vonnie for running a speakeasy in 1926.

Reba died of natural causes in 1932.

The Darke County Fair continues to draw people from both Ohio and Indiana. No further shootings, or any violent acts, have occurred during the annual fair.

A SWELL NIGHT
(ALLIANCE, 1937)

She thinks her advice is the constitution, but if she would leave that would be the solution, and don't come back no more, mother-in-law.
—Lyrics to the song "Mother-in-Law" by Ernie K-Doe

Johannes Borgwardt's rage had been simmering for just over a year, and someone was about to pay. His former mother-in-law, Ruth Cranston, with her ugly-mouthed comments and his ex-father-in-law, William, who stood quietly by, were solely responsible for the breakup of his marriage to their daughter, Evelyn. Their meddling had influenced his wife to divorce him only after two and a half years of marriage. Yes, it seemed to Johannes as he slashed through the cornfields toward the Cranston farm that muggy August evening it definitely was, as he had touted earlier in the day, "a swell night for someone to get killed whether they liked it or not."

For Johannes, meeting Evelyn had been the best thing to ever happen to him. Most of his life he lived under the rule of his domineering and reportedly physically abusive father. Immigrating to the United States from Germany in 1927 when Johannes was just thirteen, the Borgwardt family settled in Rochester, New York, where his father was a preacher at a German-Orthodox church. When Johannes learned that his father wanted him to continue in his footsteps as a German minister, Johannes bucked at the idea, much to his father's angry disproval. For the next few years, Johannes set out to make a life for himself. He held a variety of jobs, including working at a printing shop in New York and bussing tables in a

A romantic-themed postcard popular in the early 1900s. *Author's collection.*

restaurant in Hollywood, California. Eventually, perhaps wanting to be closer to his sisters, he made his way back east, where he landed a job as a farmhand on the Schoeni farm in Westville, a rural town in Columbiana County, Ohio. It was here during his twenty-first summer, in 1933, when he first laid eyes on eighteen-year-old Evelyn Cranston and his luck finally seemed to change for the better.

While attending Sunday service at Bethal Reformed Church, where his boss Fred Schoeni and family worshipped, Johannes immediately noticed the pretty brunette sitting with her family. Surprisingly, the young woman seemed interested in the handsome newcomer as well. And when Johannes made certain to introduce himself to her after services, he was delighted to learn that Evelyn and her family lived adjacent to Schoeni's farm, where he was working as a farmhand.

Within a few weeks' time, a romance between the two was in full bloom, and they were often spotted openly meeting between the two properties. Yet when William and especially Ruth, Evelyn's parents, learned of the relationship, they decided to intervene at once. Not only was Johannes an undocumented immigrant, a foreigner, but he was also a lowly farmhand who could not possibly provide for their daughter. Besides that, Evelyn, although eighteen, was still in high school and needed to concentrate on her studies and help her family around the home, not go gallivanting with a twenty-one-year-old man. Thus, much to the disappointment of the newly formed couple, Evelyn was ordered not to see Johannes.

Not surprisingly though, like many young couples, the ban on their relationship only seemed to add fuel to the fire. Soon, the pair began clandestine meetings whenever Evelyn's parents were out for the day. Luckily, both parents worked long hours at the pottery plants in nearby Sebring, leaving the couple plenty of time to pick up where they had left off. As soon as Evelyn's parents left the home, Evelyn would either phone Johannes or, even more ingeniously, would stand behind the barn and give a sharp whistle to alert that the coast was clear. This routine continued for several weeks, only adding to the thrill of the secret romance.

Yet the plan, as clever as they thought it was, was not foolproof, especially with Evelyn's protective twenty-year-old brother, William Jr., still living at home. Soon word made its way back to her parents that not only was Evelyn still seeing Johannes, but she was sneaking the fellow into the house as well. Furious now and realizing that they were losing the battle to keep the pair apart, the Cranstons sought the help of local law enforcement. But with no crime committed, as both parties were of age, there was not much that the police could offer in way of assistance other than to give Johannes a stern warning to keep off the property or be charged with trespassing.

Over the next few weeks, the Cranstons were steadfast in their determination to keep their daughter away from the young farmhand next door. Day after day, Ruth focused her attentions on Evelyn while William kept constant watch over the fields. Unfortunately, even with these concentrated efforts to put an end to the relationship, their attempts were no rival for the couple's fiery desire to be together as the vigilant parents would soon learn.

Waking before dawn one October morning in 1934, William and Ruth discovered that their daughter was missing from her bed. Not finding her in the house, they proceeded to search the barn and surrounding buildings, assuming they would find Evelyn and Johannes cuddling in some dark corner. With no sign of the pair, the Cranstons marched over to the Schoeni place, only to find that Johannes was missing as well. Apparently, the couple had run off somewhere together, leaving the Cranstons no choice but to wait helplessly for their return.

As the hours ticked by, the Cranstons planned their next course of action. Perhaps they could take Evelyn to stay with Ruth's relatives in Cincinnati. Maybe the distance would curtail the relationship and the two would eventually forget about each other. Better yet, Evelyn could potentially meet a man better suited for her while away and that would be the end of that no-good foreigner in her life. Yes, this would be the solution, and there would be nothing the two could do about it. With a newfound resolution, the Cranstons calmly stood to meet the couple, who walked hand in hand up the driveway later that evening. However, for all the parents' planning, they were not prepared for the news they were about to receive.

Sometime in the night, Evelyn and Johannes had made their way to Wellsburgh, West Virginia, the closest location that would perform a marriage involving a female under the age of twenty-one without parental consent. Apparently, all went as planned, as early the next morning, the young couple became Mr. and Mrs. Johannes Borgwardt. With the deed done and their relationship cemented by law, the two made their way back to the Cranston home to show that not only were they serious about their love for one another but they were also now married adults who could make their own choices.

When the newlyweds revealed their matrimony to William and Ruth, Evelyn's parents openly proclaimed their anger and disappointment. They made no secret that they did not approve of Johannes and had no faith in his ability to provide for their daughter, as evidenced by the fact that the newly married couple had no place to live or even stay for the night. Nonetheless, as enraged as they were, they were not about to let their daughter become homeless and allowed the pair to stay with them until other arrangements could be made.

Under the new living circumstances, tension immediately began to brew not only between the young Borgwardts and the Cranstons but between the newlyweds as well. Reportedly, Ruth expressed her unhappiness by continually making rude comments about her new son-in-law. Whenever possible, she would pull her daughter aside and reiterate that Evelyn could have done so much better for herself in the matter of securing a husband. In addition, Ruth openly made it known to her extended family and neighbors that she was not in favor of the marriage. Consequently, after several weeks of this, Evelyn began to show signs of discontentment with her decision to marry. As for Johannes, he was determined to secure a home away from his in-laws and their criticisms and was soon able to save enough money to do so as he continued to work on the neighboring farm.

Settling in Sebring in a set of small furnished rooms, the couple attempted to work on their marriage. Initially, away from the influence of Evelyn's mother, they seemed to enjoy married life, as would later be attested by neighbors they befriended in the apartment building. However, after a few months on their own, Evelyn began to sink into a depression while Johannes became more and more frustrated. To further add to their troubles, Ruth started to drop by the apartment several days a week after her shift at the pottery plant, stating that she had to wait for William to pick her up on his way home from work. During these visits, Johannes would find any excuse to leave the apartment. His absence and the effect of whatever was said about him when he was not there further strained the marriage.

Soon, Johannes's irritation grew with the situation, which he angrily voiced to Evelyn. She, too, expressed her displeasure in the marriage and went as far as to suggest a divorce. This only served to embitter Johannes more, and the cycle of arguments persisted. As the marriage continued to sour, Ruth, who witnessed the discord during her regular visits, helpfully suggested that some time apart would do the couple good. Reluctantly, Johannes agreed to let Evelyn go on a trip with her parents for a few days with hopes that his wife would miss him and change her mind about the possibility of a divorce.

On Evelyn's return, though, things seemed to go from bad to worse. Not only was Evelyn moving forward with a divorce, but she was declaring that Johannes had been a mean and nasty partner as well. At once, she removed her belongings from the apartment and moved back to her former home with her parents. Later, William reported that "Mother and I tried to get her to go back to her husband. But when she said that Johnnie had been threatening to kill her, we hired a lawyer and helped her get a divorce."

Meanwhile, Johannes alternated between pleading for Evelyn to change her mind and launching into furious demands that she return home at once. Still, no amount of begging or commanding could change Evelyn or her parents' minds. By June 1936, only after two years and eight months of marriage, the couple had officially divorced.

Immediately following the end of the marriage and after washing their hands of a nasty husband and worthless son-in-law, the Cranston family seemed to return to business as usual. Meanwhile, Johannes struggled to keep his anger in check. Furiously, he continued to work the late summer harvest, all the while making snide and often violent remarks against his former in-laws to anyone within earshot. To Johannes, William and especially Ruth were to blame for the collapse of the marriage, and as the last of the crops came down, his resentment steadily continued to go up. Fortunately, and perhaps before he snapped, Johannes decided to get as far away as possible from the situation.

Making his way back to Rochester, New York, Johannes set his mind on creating a new life for himself as well as getting over Evelyn. For the next year, he worked a variety of jobs and spent time with his sisters and their family. But as much as he tried to distract himself, Johannes continued to obsess on the divorce and his hatred for Ruth and William. Over and over, he reexamined the marriage and its breakdown, constantly replaying the offensive comments spoken against him. Neither time nor distance eased his loathing for those who were to blame for his misery. For Johannes, there seemed to be only one solution to his suffering: somebody needed to pay.

With a plan simmering in his mind, Johannes made his way back to Ohio on August 8, 1937, just a little over a year after his divorce. Checking into the Stark Hotel in Alliance, about six miles from the Cranston homestead, he made no secret of his return. Brazenly, he roamed the main streets of the town, not caring that past acquaintances, who would later become witnesses, spotted him loitering. During one of these strolls, he was certain that he saw Evelyn and Ruth, whom he believed openly snubbed him, only adding to his fury. Likewise, on the evening of August 9, he recognized

A streetcar in Alliance like the one Borgwardt used to travel between Alliance and Sebring hours before the murder. *Used with permission of Alliance Historical Society and AllianceMemory.org.*

Ruth's cousin Ellen Stahl waiting for the streetcar. She, too, paid him no mind as he cheerfully announced to her and anyone else in earshot, "It's a swell night for someone to get killed whether they like it or not." Later, Ellen explained that Johannes "always spoke like that," so she ignored his comments. Unfortunately, no one suspected that his open threats would come to fruition just a few hours later.

After his little chat with Ellen, Johannes made his way to Sebring by way of the streetcar, about a ten-minute ride east of Alliance. Once in town, he wandered around until nightfall around nine o'clock and then made his way to Fifteenth Street. From there, he followed the road to the edge of town, where it continued into the country. Even with the cover of darkness, Johannes was taking no chances. He meandered through the pastures and cornfields, avoiding the road as he approached his first stop: his previous place of employment.

At the Schoeni farm, Joahnnes quietly let himself into a small toolshed. Quickly, he located the gun that "ole man Schoeni" kept hidden for potential emergencies on the property. Next to the gun, he found several rounds of ammunition, which he scooped up and pocketed. He supposed he really only needed two bullets in this case, but there was always the chance that he could miss his targets or someone could potentially interfere. It was better to take all the supply to be on the safe side.

Stealthy now, he stepped out of the shed and continued his quest. Carefully, staying close to the barns, sheds, and cornstalks, Johannes followed the same path he used not so long ago on his secret rendezvous with Evelyn. The thought of it only enraged him more as he crept between the two properties.

Marching on, he finally could make out the outline of Cranston house. There in the darkness, hidden between the dense cornstalks, he observed the home, noting that the lights were still on, both upstairs and down. Creeping closer still, he detected someone in the lower part of the house moving about the place. Just as he recognized the silhouette of William Cranston though the window, he heard the low growl of one of the Cranstons' dogs, which, in turn, alerted the other two dogs that something was amiss. As all three dogs approached the cornfield, they began a loud cacophony, which was only amplified by the otherwise stillness of the night. With this, Johannes slunk back further into his hideout, hoping that the dogs would lose interest and back off.

Meanwhile, William Cranston, who had been readying for the night shift at the pottery plant, sighed as the dogs began their frenzied song and dance. Living in the country, it was not unusual for the animals to carry on, often barking out a warning to other creatures that moved about the property. Yet even so, as William gazed out the back window, he noticed that the pack was poised and focused on the cornfield. Whatever was out there, it had not made a run for it, as the dogs would have given chase. Instead, the object of interest stayed put, causing the dogs to continue their noisy vigil.

Knowing the dogs would not settle down on their own accord, William swung open the back screen door. As he glanced around the yard, he saw no signs of trouble. Likewise, once he called the dogs off their stance and quieted them, he could make out no sounds other than the crickets chattering to one another and the gentle swishing sound of the cornstalk leaves. Most likely the hounds had detected a deer passing through and their outburst caused the creature to freeze in fear. Ordering the dogs to retreat to their usual sleeping arrangements near the back door, William returned to the house and paused to survey the property one more time.

From his hiding place, Johannes watched his former father-in-law. At this point, he had perfect aim at the man whom he had initially planned to kill. Yet for some reason, he could not pull the trigger. For all his rage, he somehow felt an inkling of doubt. After all, William had not been the main source of the problems within the marriage. Sure, he had stood by while Ruth ran her big mouth, but the man was otherwise a decent fellow. Lowering his weapon, Johannes watched as William entered the house, pausing to hook the lock on the screen door behind him. A few minutes later, he heard the crunch of tires as William backed down the driveway on his way to work.

Once the taillights faded into the night, Johannes made his way to the edge of the yard. In what would be only one of few efforts to cover his tracks, he slipped off his shoes. He had once read that criminals were often identified by their shoeprints. Not wanting to take that chance, he placed his shoes near the back stoop and continued toward one of the downstairs windows, the only room with the light still on inside.

At this point, the dogs apparently recognized him from his brief stay with the family and made no attempt to warn him from their turf. Had they continued in their earlier complaints, perhaps the occupants in the home would have stood a chance against the danger that lurked just outside the residence. Even if the animals had given a friendly whine or jumped on their visitor, the downstairs occupant would have heard them considering that the screened-in window was open to allow for the night breeze. Unfortunately, the guardians made no attempt to interact with the familiar figure as he proceeded to crouch below the window.

If Johannes gave any pause before his next action, it was only to still his pounding heart. In his mind, there was no turning back, and as he rose just enough to see into the window, his blood turned cold. There, comfortably lying in her bed and reading a book was Ruth Cranston. Just the sight of her, seemingly content with her life and oblivious to the pain she had caused, was enough for Johannes to slowly level the shotgun on the windowsill. Just as she flipped to the next page, Johannes pulled the trigger, emitting a deafening blast that reverberated through the stillness of the night.

Blinking away the dust caused by the explosion, Johannes ascertained that the job was complete. As the agitated dogs now jumped and pawed around his legs, he could clearly see that he had succeeded in this task. The eyes that had once darkened with disgust at the mere sight of him and the mouth that had poisoned Evelyn against him were a bloodied, mangled mess, as he had hit his target directly in the face. It was evident that Ruth would not be meddling in his life again.

While the dogs began to recover from the upheaval, Johannes stood back from the house. He waited for any sign of movement from within the home. Certainly, Evelyn or her brother, William Jr., would be home, since it had to be just after midnight. They should have sprung their feet with the commotion that occurred just below their own open windows. But as the minutes passed, it seemed that any other occupants of the home were unaware or undisturbed by the events, so it made sense that they did not hear the tear of the screen as Joahnnes shoved the shotgun through it and lifted the tiny metal hook from its latch.

Making his way through the home where he had spent the first few months of his marriage, he stopped by the kitchen phone, where he removed the receiver from its cradle. Next, he easily found the stairway leading to the upstairs rooms. Standing just outside of Evelyn's bedroom, he listened for any movement. Hearing nothing but the sound of his own breathing, he slowly turned the knob and felt around the wall for the light switch. With a gentle click, the light illuminated the room and revealed the small form of someone peacefully sleeping in the bed.

Whatever his intended next steps were, the plan was forgotten as Johannes stood frozen in the doorway watching his ex-wife. If only her parents had stayed out of it, he could be lying beside her in their own home far away from this mess. Mesmerized by being in her presence and the bittersweet what-ifs, he moved closer to her bedside. Knowing he probably had only a precious few minutes left before he needed to flee, he knelt to have one final look at her. Suddenly, just as he raised his hand to stroke her hair, the flash of headlights bounced off the wall.

Springing to action, propelled from his momentary lovesick oblivion back to the situation, he quickly snapped off the light. Listening intently, he could make out the sound of a car approaching the Cranston home. On his return trip back down the stairs, he made no attempt to conceal the noise as he took the steps two at a time, galloping through the back of the house and practically falling out of the back door. Just as the headlights cut through the yard as the car turned into the driveway, Johannes blindly grabbed his shoes and darted back into the cornfield. Hearing the distinct sound of car door slamming, he thrashed his way through the stalks, not knowing if William, a neighbor, or worse, the police, were on his tail.

Ignorantly, Johannes had not gotten much further than the murder business during the planning stages of his revenge plot. As he stumbled disoriented through the darkness, he attempted to formulate the next steps. First things first, he needed to rid himself of the weapon, and returning it to its rightful owner was out of the question. Just as he considered burying it in the thicket that he had entered, he noticed the shining surface of water just yards from him. Somehow, in his haste to escape capture, he had

Railroad tracks leading into Alliance. Borgwardt followed the tracks in an attempt to stay hidden after he committed murder. *Used with permission of Alliance Historical Society and AllianceMemory.org.*

traveled about one mile southeast from the Cranstons' home, arriving at Westville Lake. Although he had initially intended to head northwest back toward Alliance, he used the mistake to his advantage as he stood on the dam and tossed the weapon into the water.

Now aware of his location, after a few minutes to catch his breath, he began the trek back toward his hotel. Traveling through the fields, he soon located the Stark Electric tracks and followed the line for several miles. Hours later, he made his way to Lake Park, where he found he could go no further due to his exhaustion. With just a couple hours before daybreak, Johannes stretched out on a park bench and fell into a peaceful sleep.

Meanwhile, the scene at the Cranstons was anything but peaceful. Just after midnight, William Jr. had driven toward home after a late work shift. As he made his way down the country lane, he was surprised to see Evelyn's bedroom light still on. It was unusual that she or his mother would be up so late. Strangely, by the time he reached the driveway, the light was off.

A postcard of Lake Shore Park near Alliance where Borwardt slept the night of his crime. *From the Columbus Metropolitan Library Image Collections.*

Concerned that something was amiss, William Jr. scanned the house for any signs of problems. Alarmingly, just as his headlights cut through the yard, he was certain that he saw a figure dash across the backyard.

Without hesitation, William Jr. exited the car and ran toward the backyard. The dogs, surprisingly more interested in William's return instead of the stranger on the property, raced to meet him, impeding any chance of William catching the trespasser. Pushing past his welcome party, he turned toward the back door. With a sickening sensation in his stomach, he noticed the ripped screen door and dangling latch.

Bolting into the house, he called out to his mother and sister as he made his way to his parents' bedroom. The only response he heard was a soft moaning coming from Ruth and William's downstairs bedroom. Flicking on the light, he tried to make sense of the horrid scene before him.

Within the next hour, William Sr. returned to the homestead after receiving a frantic phone call from his son explaining that something terrible had happened at the home. An hour after that, Columbiana County Sheriff Harry Gosney and three deputies arrived on the scene, where they were met by William and his two children, who seemed to be in shock as they explained that Ruth had been killed. As Sheriff Gosney assessed the scene, he quickly realized that he was indeed dealing with a murder investigation based on the family's statements, the torn screen, and the almost faceless dead body.

As the deputies fanned out to search the vicinity, the sheriff scoured the home and yard for any clues. He did not have to look far, for under the bedroom window, he immediately found a spent shotgun shell. Shining a light closer to the ground, he also noticed the impression of what looked like a bare footprint, and he called for a plaster cask to be made. He surmised that the murderer most likely had lain in wait somewhere on the property and then crept quietly to the window, where he proceeded to shoot the unsuspecting Ruth as she lay reading in her bed.

By daybreak, the sheriff had secured the name of a potential suspect after questioning the family. By late morning, he had learned that not only had Johannes Borgwardt been seen loitering about town, but he had openly made threats concerning the Cranston family just the day prior. Likewise, he was able to trace Borgwardt to the Stark Hotel in Alliance after word spread around the small town of Sebring. If this was indeed his man, the ex-husband had not made much of an attempt to conceal his plans or his whereabouts. In fact, it almost seemed too easy that the suspect was hiding out in a nearby hotel that he openly checked into under his real name. Even more surprising, when Sheriff Gosney and Chief Harry Stark of Alliance inquired at the hotel, they learned that Borgwardt had returned to his room around 5:00 a.m. and had not been seen leaving since then.

Pounding on the hotel door, the detectives were greeted by a groggy-looking young man. Whether confused by his unexpected visitors or just nervous at the sight the of the policemen, Johannes blurted out his name and proceeded to ask if they were there concerning "those bad checks that I passed." When the officers explained that they were there to ask him about the murder of Ruth Cranston, he quickly denied any knowledge. However, once he was taken to the station and grilled for a few hours, he eventually confessed to shooting Ruth. By the early afternoon of August 11, the confessed murderer of Ruth Cranston was on his way to the Columbiana County Jail to await his booking.

Over the next few months, Prosecutor Karl Stouffer dug deep into the history between the Cranstons and Johannes Borgwardt. In Borgwardt's original confession, he admitted that he blamed William and Ruth for the decline and ultimate ending of the marriage. He also explained that he had returned to Ohio with the intention of getting revenge on his former in-laws. Detailing his crime in almost step-by-step fashion, he related how he had secured the gun and proceeded to the farm, where he positioned the weapon through Ruth's screen and blasted her with it. Allegedly showing no signs of remorse during his confession and feeling justified, he stated that he "he would gladly do it again." For the prosecution, it seemed as though they would have an open-and-shut case, proving that not only was Bogwardt guilty but the murder was premeditated as well. With that, they would be seeking the death penalty.

Conversely, when the trial commenced in late November, Borgwardt's defense team, made up of attorney H.L. McCarthy and attorney Charles Boyd, argued that the accused was confused and disoriented when signing the confession. In fact, Borgwardt would be pleading guilty by way of insanity and the defense planned to prove it. He had no recollection of pulling the trigger or the aftermath, including fleeing the scene. Additionally, his confession at police headquarters was all a blur thanks to his mental instability. When the defense brought in Dr. Burke, supervising doctor at the Newburgh Asylum in Cleveland, he explained that Borgwardt "wouldn't know right from wrong and has no stamina to resist temptation," as reported in the *East Liverpool Evening Review*. This condition, which the good doctor described as "paranoia marked by gradual impairment of intellect accompanied by delusion," could be attributed to a blow to the head that Borgwardt received during childhood as attested by his sisters, who described the event in detail to the court.

Opposingly, the prosecution attempted to show that Borgwardt indeed knew exactly what he was doing and precisely how he would do it. When Johannes took the stand, they scrutinized his character, pointing out that he had been a "mean husband" and that is why Evelyn had left him. Evidence presented included the shotgun retrieved from the lake and casts of footprints found at the scene. Likewise, the entire jury was loaded up on a bus and transported to the Cranston home, where they were able to better visualize the scene where a defenseless woman was shot without warning by an enraged madman.

All the while, Johannes, showing emotion only when he described his love for Evelyn, continued to explain that he had never meant to kill anyone and would not hurt his ex-wife that way. Accordingly, the defense produced over a dozen locals, including church members and neighbors, who testified to Borgwardt's overall good character before the marriage to Evelyn. On top of that, his sisters insisted that in addition to a head wound, he had been severely beaten by their father, suggesting that he should be shown some mercy, as he was most assuredly mentally unstable due to his past.

For five days, jurors listened as both sides presented evidence and testimony about the events leading up to the murder and the murder itself. In the end, after two and a half hours of deliberation, the jury found Johannes Borgwardt guilty of the premeditated murder of his former mother-in-law. The penalty for his crime, as sentenced by Judge W. Frank Lones, was life imprisonment with a recommendation of mercy after sixteen years.

While Johannes served his time, Evelyn attempted to move on with her life. Unfortunately, married life seemed to come with many hurdles. Soon after the trial, she married a local man by the name of Otto Buehler. They had two children together: a daughter named Ruth and a son. Eventually, they divorced, and in 1951, she married James Danner. That marriage ended in divorce as well. In her early fifties, Evelyn married her fourth husband, Robert Missmer, and settled into a life dedicated to community organizations and improvement projects in Lehigh County, Pennsylvania. Evelyn passed away in 1993 at the age of seventy-six.

As for Johannes, he spent the first decade of his incarceration at the Ohio Penitentiary in Columbus. Later, he was transported to the London Prison Farm, a branch unit of the Ohio Penitentiary for prisoners demonstrating good behavior. During his years in confinement, Borgwardt was reportedly a model prisoner and took advantage of an education program, completing several courses. In 1953, after serving fifteen years, thirty-nine-year-old Johannes Borgwardt was granted parole. Shortly after his release, he met and married a widowed woman from Kentucky, and the two eventually moved to St. Petersburg, Florida, in the 1960s. Johannes lived a quiet life and was passionate about foreign missions, working and volunteering for the United World Missions. He also served as Sunday School superintendent at his local church. At the time of his is death in 1999, he had been married to his second wife for forty-five years.

No further trouble with a mother-in-law was ever reported.

A PHANTOM LOVE
(CANTON, 1928)

Women are motivated by a love drive, and that makes them look at everything that takes place as a personal matter between themselves and somebody else.... They lack the impulse to keep their emotional acts with the smooth bounds of convention.

—Professor William Marston, from the article "Science Says Woman's Love Drive Goads Her to Violent Crime," Evansville Courier and Press, 1929

From the outside looking in, perhaps through the window of a darkened front porch, it seemed that thirty-five-year-old Vernard Fearn had it all. As he pressed his napkin to his mouth after another fine supper lovingly prepared by Mary, his devoted wife of ten years, he nodded his approval to her. Seated to his side in their newly built home was his nine-year-old daughter, Katheryn, who clearly adored her daddy based on the way she giggled at whatever it was he was saying. A quick glance to the right of the porch, and anyone would conclude that business was going well, as attested by the meticulously kept delivery truck with its professionally painted advertisement for "Vernard Fearn, Coal Delivery, Waco, Ohio" on the side. Yes, there in that cozy little house in a quiet hamlet outside of Canton, Ohio, the handsome family man sat content in his idyllic life. Certainly, anyone would conclude based on that picturesque scene that Vernard Fearn was nearly perfect. Anyone, that is, except for the figure that stood just outside the front door preparing to blast him and his carefully protected façade into smithereens.

A romantic-themed postcard popular in the early 1900s. *Author's collection.*

When the knock at the door came at 6:20 p.m. on the December 6, 1928, Mary Fearn assumed that it was one of her husband's many customers coming to pay for a recent delivery of coal. Over the last year, Vern's business had been flooded with orders with deliveries for not only their small village but also clients in Canton. Thus, when the visitor, a petite woman, asked to speak to Vernard, again Mary thought it was business as usual. Always a polite hostess, Mary asked the visitor to come inside, but the woman refused, stating that she would rather wait on the porch. Turning back toward the dining room and her daughter, she left Vern to deal with the guest. It was not until a deafening series of blasts reverberated through the entire house that Mary realized that something was horribly wrong. As if in slow motion, she watched as her husband stumbled back into the house while the popping continued. Mary gasped as Vernard then fell to the floor, stains of blood immediately seeping through his shirt near his chest, neck, and side.

If the first few seconds of the incident seemed to occur in slow motion, the next few minutes were a whirlwind as Mary tried to process what was happening. Although the gunshots had stopped just as abruptly as they started, the ringing in Mary's ears persisted as she called out for Katheryn. Thankfully, the girl had had the good sense to take cover behind the front room chair. In the next instance, as Mary turned toward the front door, she caught a blur of motion as a figure ran from the porch and out into the darkness. Quickly slamming the door closed, Mary ran to her husband, who lay moaning on the floor.

Perching by his side and lightly stroking his face, Mary realized that Vern was attempting to speak. "I'm a goner," he mumbled softly as she squeezed his hand. Trying not to sob as she realized that Vern was, in fact, dying, she continued to gently rock her husband in her arms as he struggled to communicate his final words. With one last burst of breath, Vern murmured, "I don't know that woman. I've never seen her in my life," just as he slipped away.

Minutes later, when Chief Deputy George Daily of Stark County received a frantic call concerning a possible murder in Waco, he was perplexed. The caller had to be mistaken. Certainly, a farming or hunting accident could have occurred out there in the quiet village about three miles southeast of downtown Canton, but it seemed improbable that it was an actual homicide. Regardless, Daily contacted Coroner T.A. McQuate to assist, as there was some type of fatality, whether accidental or intentional, involved based on the caller's hysteria. A half hour later, after seeing the bloody body riddled with six of the eight expended bullets, the chief no longer had doubts about the possibility of a homicide in tiny little Waco.

Opening an investigation immediately, Daily interviewed anyone available at or near the crime scene. Based on Mary Fearn's report, the shooter was a woman. She stated that the woman did seem somewhat familiar, but she could not place her. She also informed Daily that her husband claimed to have never seen the woman in his life. Next, the Fearns' neighbor reported that she too saw a female figure fleeing down the hill seconds after she heard the gunshots. Following that lead, Daily made a visit to the Rite-o-Way Inn at the bottom of the hill, about three hundred yards from the Fearns' home. Here, he learned that an unknown woman had arrived on the Canton-Waynesburg bus around 6:15 p.m. She had disembarked but returned about fifteen minutes later to catch the bus back to Canton. More curious was that the inn proprietor stated that the same woman had been there the previous night, not once but twice. On both nights, she had gotten off the bus, walked in the direction of the Fearns' home, and returned a few minutes later to the bus.

Corroborating the story of the mysterious visitor, the bus driver distinctly remembered the woman as well. His thoughts were that she was working for the bus company, and her strange behavior could be attributed to the fact that she was secretly reporting back to headquarters on the busing operations. Both evenings, she had boarded and departed the bus at the McKinley Hotel stop in downtown Canton. On both evenings, she had kept to herself, avoiding eye contact and speaking only to the driver on her last trip, asking about bus connections to Lorain, a suburb of Cleveland. Likewise, other passengers remembered seeing the mysterious rider as well, describing her as a small, attractive woman, probably around twenty-two, wearing a stylish blue chinchilla coat and a furry black hat.

By Friday morning, the mysterious murder of Vernard Fearn had made the papers. Referring to the murderess as the "Phantom-Flapper Killer," the media capitalized on the eerie nature of the crime, which was not difficult to do considering the strange details that were presented. First, the killer appeared on the Fearns' doorstep on an otherwise ordinary evening and proceeded to shoot her victim in front of his family. She then calmly boarded the bus as though simply traveling from Point A to Point B, and then, most hauntingly, she seemed to disappear into thin air. Second, after a ballistics examination, Stark County Sheriff Ed Gibson determined that the murder weapon was an antiquated gun that was prevalent decades prior among professional hitmen. To obtain bullets for the gun almost would be impossible in 1929. Again, it was as if the killer had indeed transported from another dimension or time, strengthening the ghostly angle of the ordeal and making front-page news across the country as other media outlets sold the chilling story to delighted audiences. Last, the bold, calloused killer had not only murdered someone in cold blood, but apparently—and according to initial reports—she had also chosen an upstanding family man as her victim, which only a heartless being could do.

For investigators, questioning family, friends, and neighbors offered little in way of tracking down a suspect or producing a motive. When people in Vernard Fearn's inner circle learned the tragic news of how he was gunned down at his own home in front of his family, they were genuinely shocked. Vern was not only a model husband and father, but he was reportedly a fine businessman and faithful churchgoer as well. Everyone from his customers to his family and friends attested to his hard work ethic as well as his friendly, fun-loving demeanor. To have any enemies at all, especially one that would kill him in such a cold-blooded manner, seemed completely far-fetched. Even his mother, Emma Fearn, attested to Vern's gentle disposition, explaining that "he was always a mother's boy and carried his troubles and woes to his mother for guidance, until the day he died," as reported in the *Canton Repository*.

Although it appeared that Vern was a respectable man, Sheriff Gibson could not shake the feeling that they were missing something. Analyzing the murder, it was clear to him that premeditation had been involved. After all, the killer had plenty of time to reconsider her motives on her three known bus rides out to Waco. Her efforts were focused and bold, suggesting that she had a vendetta against her victim that she was determined to carry out one way or another. Operating on the fact the killer was indeed female, Gibson turned the investigation to the possibility that Vernard might have had secretive encounters with a woman or women not known to his closest family and friends. If so, one of the most logical places to visit would be any of the dance halls that Fearn was known to frequent.

Inquiring at the dance halls and interviewing regular patrons of the establishments, Gibson learned that his victim was quite the ladies' man on the dance floor. Handsome and jovial, Vernard easily acquired numerous dance partners, becoming flirty and sometimes handsy with the girls. Even with the party crowd, a known married man openly fraternizing with women raised some eyebrows. Although not a crime, Fearns's late-night behavior painted a slightly different picture of the respectable husband,

and Gibson had some questions, particularly for a few local gals who reportedly spent time with Fearn both on and off the dance floor.

For Gibson, one woman, a local stenographer, was of particular interest, as rumor had it that she and Fearn may have had an affair. She confessed that the pair had gone on a date, but that was all that had occurred between the two. As far as the night of the murder, the woman produced an airtight alibi, and she was cleared as a suspect.

Continuing to work on information gathered from the dance-hall crowd, Gibson followed a lead to the 200 block of Newton Street, not far from the McKinley Hotel. According to witnesses, Fearn's work truck, which proudly displayed his name on the side, had been seen parked outside an apartment that was rented by a couple. The visits supposedly took place while the husband was working, according to observant neighbors. Speaking to the landlord, Gibson learned that the couple, Mr. and Mrs. Heldman, had moved to the Cleveland area about two months prior to the murder, which left Gibson nothing to go on other than the confirmation that Fearn had visited someone at that location on several occasions.

As the investigation took on more of a salacious nature over the following week, Fearn's family, especially his mother, was quick to defend her son's good name. According to an interview published in the *Canton Repository*, Emma and Vernard's sister did not believe any of the gossip concerning his relationships with other women. They insisted that "the boy was raised Christian, raised to be truthful, coached to revere womanhood and to be a loving husband and father. They have no fear in their hearts that Vern was philandering with strange women in Canton or elsewhere. They do not believe the stories that Vern was a two-woman man. They do not believe he was faithless."

Frustratingly, after conducting dozens of interviews, chasing several leads, and digging deep into Fearn's personal life, Sheriff Gibson and his team were not any closer to tracking down the killer than they were the night of the murder. Although it was apparent that Fearn had an assortment of lady friends on the side, finding one with a motive strong enough to kill him was proving difficult. Consequently, on the one-week anniversary of the crime, Gibson, sitting alone in his office reviewing the case yet another time, was slowly coming to terms with the notion that the murder may go unsolved. Like her moniker, the Phantom-Flapper Killer, suggested, the murderess seemed to have slipped into the dark unknown. As it was, when he heard the frantic honking of an automobile just outside his office at 6:00 p.m. on December 13, he had no inclination that his phantom slayer had arrived on his doorstep almost to the hour and the day of her crime.

Rushing outside, the sheriff encountered a panic-stricken man standing half out of the driver's side door. Frantically gesticulating, the driver directed Gibson toward the passenger seat. There, slumped against the door, was a barely conscious woman. On further inspection, he could see the tell-tale sign of a wound to her chest as blood seeped through the material of her thick chinchilla coat. Without hesitation, Gibson hopped into the back seat and yelled for the driver to proceed to Mercy Hospital a few miles from the station.

En route, Gibson learned that Wilbur Heldman and his wife, Margaret, now struggling to breathe in the front seat, had driven from Lorain to Canton, a nearly eighty-mile drive, when Margaret had pulled out a gun and shot herself as they neared the Canton city limits. As Heldman navigated toward the hospital, he explained that he had been transporting his wife to Canton so that she could confess to the murder of her lover, Vernard Fearn. Listening intently to the details provided by Wilbur on the frenzied drive and given the current situation, Gibson deduced that one or both Heldmans had been involved in Fearn's murder. Unfortunately, he would never have the chance to interrogate Margaret, as she slipped into unconsciousness and then death within the hour of her arrival to the hospital.

Over the next couple of days, Gibson and his team pressed Wilbur Heldman for information. The bereaved husband explained how he learned about Margaret's betrayal and how he became suspicious when he heard about Fearn's murder via the newspapers. Although Heldman was quite forthcoming with details of the affair and his keen detective skills, he was initially evasive about his relationship with the alleged murderer, his deceased wife. Slowly, though, he began to reveal more about the marriage and the breakdown thereof. As Heldman shared his story, the team found themselves attempting to untangle a web of marital discord and infidelity stemming back to the early days of the Heldmans' marriage.

Wilbur reported that he met Margaret soon after her high school graduation in August 1927, when she arrived from Debois, Pennsylvania, and began work at Zollinger's Department Store as a ribbon cutter. Although he was twenty-six years old, the two were instantly attracted to each other and began a whirlwind courtship that resulted in marriage just three weeks after meeting. From there, they moved into two furnished rooms on Newton Street and attempted to settle into married life. As

Left: Margaret Heldman, suspected of killing her lover, 1928. *From Acme Newspictures Inc.*

Right: Wilbur Heldman, who convinced his wife to confess to murder, 1928. *From Acme Newspictures Inc.*

Margaret took on her domestic roles as a newlywed, however, Wilbur noted that her pre-marriage enthusiasm for the relationship was quickly replaced with complaints and foul moods, which led to heated arguments between the two.

As the months turned into a year, the couple fell into a pattern of fiery spats and passionate reconciliations, one of which resulted in a pregnancy. Like many young couples, the idea of a baby brought with it a promise of a new beginning and the assumption that the marriage would improve once the bundle of joy arrived. Plus, the couple was planning to relocate to Lorain, which should also offer a fresh start. However, by the time baby Emmit was born in September 1928, the couple's unhappiness had become even more pronounced; the additional responsibility of caring for an infant seemed to add to Margaret's disdain toward domestic life. In fact, according to Wilbur, Margaret proved incompetent as a mother, forcing them to leave the infant with Margaret's sister in Canton while they attempted to work on their crumbling marriage in Lorain.

Shortly after their move, with the word *divorce* often thrown between the two, Wilbur realized that the marriage was truly on the brink of collapse, as attested by a letter written by Margaret to her sister that he found. In the letter, dated November 2, Margaret wrote,

> *Wilbur and I are having trouble again and I guess it will be for the last time. I know I told a lot* [of] *lies to you and him and I guess I might as well tell you the truth before he does. You remember when we lived at Hubbard's and we all went out to dance at Smile Inn and we met Mr. and Mrs. Fearn. I danced with Mr. Fearn and we made a date and I met him at the West End a couple of nights later. I told you I was going to a show with the girls at Zollinger's but we went for a ride and x x x x.*
>
> *Wilbur has found it out and is going to get a divorce so it will come out then so that is why I am telling you of this.*

Naturally, the letter and its contents only led to additional arguments over the next few weeks. Margaret responded by escaping to her sister's home in Canton on December 3. On her return five days later on December 7, she offered clipped one-word answers when Wilbur inquired about how her visit had gone. In fact, she seemed even more distant than before, which only solidified in Wilbur's mind that they were at the end of the road. Shockingly, the following day, his marital problems would seem insignificant compared to what he was about to discover concerning his wife.

While skimming the paper the following Saturday evening as Margaret worked in the kitchen, his eyes were drawn to an article titled "Gunwoman Still Sought for Waco Man's Murder." As he read the article, his heartbeat quickened at the general description of the murderess and the time and place of the crime, but it was the type of weapon that was used that made him catch his breath. For Wilbur owned one of the rare .380 Colts described in the paper, one of the finest pieces in his collection. With this, Wilbur sprang to his feet and called to Margaret.

Entering the kitchen, he showed his wife the article and calmly stated, "I think you did this." She immediately replied, "You are crazy," and turned back to her work as if to show that the notion was so absurd that it had no effect on her. Not ready to let it go, he asked, "Where's my gun?" to which she flippantly retorted, "Why ask me? Isn't it on the shelf?"

After checking and finding the gun undisturbed, Wilbur continued to mull the situation over in his mind. Based on the article, the description of the shooter matched Margaret to a tee. Not only that, but the murderer was seen sporting a blue chinchilla coat. To his knowledge, his wife owned only one coat, a blue chinchilla. Second, according to the letter he had found, Margaret had at least one date with Fearn, establishing a connection between the two. Nevertheless, the letter revealed no inclination of Margaret holding any resentment toward her lover. Last, although she indicated that she was unconcerned about the gun or its location, Wilbur knew that she was quite good with guns, as he had taught her how to shoot back when she at least feigned some interest in his hobbies.

Over the next few days, Margaret robotically attended to her household duties while Wilbur observed her for any hint of guilt. Meanwhile, he meticulously combed through newspaper articles concerning the "Phantom-Flapper Killer." While the reports indicated that the police were no closer to finding the crazed gunwoman, Wilbur became more assured that he knew her identity with each new clue revealed in the papers. Even still, the notion that Margaret could kill someone intentionally was hard for him to believe, causing him to hesitate over confronting her again. However, all that changed when Wilbur found what he believed was his wife's admission to the crime.

While preparing to take out the trash on December 13, Wilbur noticed a crumpled piece of paper with Margaret's handwriting. Dated December 2, the note stated the following:

> *I am leaving out of your life forever and I truly am sorry for all the trouble I have caused you, and rather than try to go through the rest of my life under a lie I am taking this means to tell you the truth. I can't face you and tell you this, so I am leaving this to explain the thing you don't know. He has made my life a hell of earth.*
>
> *He came to our home when we were living in Canton and threatened to expose me if I didn't do what he wanted me to do. The day you kicked me out because I was there standing with him was one of the times, and you didn't even know him. I don't think you have ever met him. I can't stand the worry any longer and can't bear to be away from my baby. So I do hope you can forgive me and give the baby a good home. Love him even if you don't love me for I truly do love you.*
> *Margaret*
>
> *P.S. Please do not tell my mother.*

At last, Wilbur had the final piece in the puzzle. Although all the signs had pointed to Margaret, Wilbur could not quite accept the fact that she was the killer, as there seemed to be no justification behind it. Sure, there had been an extramarital affair, but he could not fathom why it culminated in murder. Revealingly, the letter had explained just that. Apparently, Fearn had held the indiscretion over Margaret, leading her into a downward spiral with, in her mind, only one way out.

With this clarification, Wilbur knew what he had to do. Immediately, he approached his wife and explained that he was certain of what she had done and she needed to confess to the authorities. Surprisingly, Margaret made no attempt to deny her transgressions and quietly asked what he thought would happen to her after her confession. When Wilbur stated that she would be punished to the fullest for her crime, Margaret began to stall for time, asking if they could wait until the next morning to go to the police. Not wanting to lose his resolve, Wilbur insisted that she get her coat at once.

At some point, Wilbur made the decision that it would be logical to head to the Canton Police Department, as Chief Gibson and his team were handling the case. Thus, while on the nearly eighty-mile drive from Lorain, Wilbur had plenty of time to continue to question Margaret for further explanation regarding not only the murder but also the affair with Fearn.

As Margaret stared off into the distance, she explained that before she had met Wilbur, she had been introduced to Vern and his wife at one of the all-night dance halls in Canton. Vern had asked her to dance, which she accepted. After the first encounter, the two began the pattern of meeting at the halls and dancing together into the wee hours of the night even after she had married Wilbur. Soon, though, this harmless fraternizing led to a disaster from which she felt could not escape.

According to Margaret, sometime in the year prior to the murder, Vern had offered her a ride from the Canton Public Library. Trusting him and a little thrilled with the idea of sitting beside him in his fancy truck, Margaret readily agreed. Much to her confusion, Vern proceeded to leave the city limits and head toward the rural countryside. Here, the real Vernard Fearn revealed the monster that he was as he forced himself on a defenseless Margaret. Afterward, showing no remorse for what he had done, he drove her back to town, all the while threatening to tell Wilbur of their encounter. He would insist that it was consensual based on their public dates at the dance halls.

And so began the nightmare for Margaret over the following months. On numerous occasions, Vern would appear at her doorstep, always when Wilbur was away, and have his way with her. Too ashamed and scared, Margaret remained powerless against her attacker and stayed silent. Even after the Heldmans moved to Lorain, she was unable to escape the torment, as Fearn continued to threaten to expose her to the world. Finally, in early December, she could take no more and came up with a plan to put an end to her misery. She would kill not only Fearn but also herself. She claimed that the first letter Wilbur had found was not just a simple goodbye to him—it was intended to be found after she killed Fearn and took her own life.

Margaret alleged that she had initially planned to go to the Fearn home, where she would kill her tormentor and then herself. Yet when she began shooting, she could not stop, which explained the overkill that lodged six of the eight bullets in Fearn. Her intention was to turn the gun on herself, but she quickly realized that she had emptied it. With her original plan now foiled, she made her way back to downtown Canton on the bus. Not being able to face her sister, she decided to book a room in Akron at the Bond Hotel while awaiting her fate, which she assumed would come in the way of policemen beating down the door.

Listening to the details of his wife's ordeal as they neared Canton, Wilbur unsympathetically explained that she would most likely receive the death penalty. Still staring straight ahead, Margaret insisted that Wilbur promise to take care of the baby. It was then, just as he assured her of the child's care and they crossed the Canton city limits, that Margaret abruptly shifted in her seat. In a blink of an eye, she pulled out the gun from her inside coat pocket, pointed it toward her chest, and pulled the trigger.

As Wilbur reiterated the details that he had learned on that fateful drive, he neatly tied together the loose ends of this horrific story. Yes, there had been a murder and now a heartbreaking suicide, but he was just as ready as the investigators for the case to come to an end so he could begin the grieving process and attend to his son's care. With Chief Gibson and his team satisfied, though deeply saddened, they assumed the case was now closed. What they did not realize was that the story, and all its salacious details, would consume the community and leave some questioning the entire investigation.

The next day, newspapers across the country ran the story of Margeret, who may or may not have been a willing partner, and her lover, who was shot dead for his part in it. Whether Margaret was a jealous woman scorned or someone who was justified in her actions was up for public debate. Meanwhile, the only consistency was the portrayal of the third person in the triangle, and that was the blindsided husband, Willbur. Anyone could sympathize with the poor widower who learned of his wife's infidelity, listened to her confession to murder, and then watched helplessly as she killed herself. If nothing else, at least the ordeal was over, and he could finally move on. Conversely, and much to the dismay of Wilbur, Margaret's family was not so quick to accept Wilbur's account of the tragedies, insisting that investigators reexamine the case.

Much of the family's complaints centered on Wilbur's knowledge of the affair and his role in her suicide. They asserted that Wilbur had been well aware of the relationship between Margaret and Fearn and he possibly forced her to write her confession letters to her family and him. Likewise, when he realized that Margaret had killed Fearn, he used the information as a form of revenge for the affair, taunting her that she would receive the death sentence. As a result, she was led to take her own life due to fear that was heavily compounded by Wilbur's verbal abuse. Last, the family pointed out that Margaret may have survived the bullet had she been driven straight to the hospital instead of to the police station.

After law enforcement reevaluated the case and took the family's account into consideration, Wilbur Heldman was arrested as a possible witness to the death of both his wife and Vernard Fearn. This charge was eventually dropped in exchange for the more serious offense of "moral murder," similar to a modern-day second-degree manslaughter charge. In an affidavit, Coroner McQuate stated that because of Heldman's "inhuman course the night of her death, if nothing more, she [his wife] was compelled to turn that gun upon herself." His primary evidence was Wilbur's own account of telling his wife while en route to Canton that "she was headed for the electric chair."

As the weeks turned into months while Wilbur awaited his fate in the Stark County Jail, prosecution could not produce witnesses or any other concrete evidence to bring to a grand jury. Thus, four months after the death of his wife, Wilbur Heldman was set free. Two years later, in 1932, Wilbur married Slyvia Davis from Akron and had three children with her, but he eventually left her and the children. He did not secure custody of baby Emmit.

BEHIND CLOSED DOORS
(CLEVELAND, 1916)

When Louis Bianchetti and Dolores Evans met for the first time, it was not love at first sight. In fact, love, even the prospect of it, was never the intention for either party. Instead, each had their own agenda that night that had nothing to do with affection. For Louis, his intentions were straightforward: he would pay as little as possible for her services and then quietly skirt back home before his morning shift. For Dolores, a quick hustle job would be set into motion. She would be compensated for her time and then some whether she fulfilled her duties or not. Neither realized until it was much too late that death lurked just behind closed doors.

The evening of January 11, 1916, started out routine for twenty-five-year-old Louis. After working his shift as the recently promoted second chef at the prestigious Cleveland Athletic Club, he made his way to his previous place of employment, the popular Roma Restaurant. There he chatted with his former boss while he downed several beers. As the crowd thinned, Louis decided to head a few blocks over to where there was always bound to be a party, even on a Tuesday night.

When he entered the Chinese Republic restaurant, known for its round-the-clock, anything-goes atmosphere, several pairs of eyes were on him. Remarkably handsome with his floppy sandy-brown hair and twinkling eyes, the well-groomed Louis was accustomed to turning heads wherever he went. Therefore, he was not surprised when he was approached by a man offering to introduce Louis to a couple of young ladies.

A romantic-themed postcard popular in the early 1900s. *Author's collection.*

As for nineteen-year-old Dolores Evans, her evening was quite routine as well. After attempting to drum up business in a few of their regular local haunts, Dolores and her colleagues Clare Dillie and George Pierce decided to work the all-night Chinese joint, where they usually had luck setting up a job or two. It was not long before they spotted an easy, well-dressed mark proudly flashing a thick wad of cash for all to admire. From there, it was standard operating procedure as they made their move.

Within minutes, George Pierce had slipped into the seat next to Louis Bianchetti and struck up a friendly conversation. The now-relaxed Louis, somewhere between drinks six and seven, offered to buy Pierce a round, affording the guy yet another glance at the stack of bills. It was at this point that Pierce silently gave the signal for the girls to approach the bar area located close to the men's table.

First, Clara Dillie, just seventeen years old, sauntered by the pair. Nudging Louis in a buddy-buddy manner, Pierce pointed out the girl and asked if he would like to meet her. Louis, realizing that the girl was quite young, shook his head "no." As if by magic, Dolores appeared. Again, Pierce kindly offered to introduce Louis to his pretty acquaintance, this time earning a mumbled "I don't care" from Louis. With this, the plan quickly moved forward as the group reassembled at a private table.

After quick introductions, the conversation, most likely laced with seductive innuendos, transitioned to plans for the rest of the evening. Somewhere in the mix of flirty remarks and free-flowing booze, Dolores and Louis decided to move their party to a more private setting.

Outside the restaurant, Louis attempted to persuade Dolores to accompany him to his apartment. However, Dolores insisted that she would be more comfortable at the Hotel Perry just a few blocks away. As they made their way down Prospect Avenue, shivering in the frosty air, both happily anticipated the way the next few hours would go. Unfortunately, as they checked into room 19 under the name of Mr. and Mrs. Lou White, neither knew that only one of them would survive the night.

The next morning, Detective Captain Alfred Walker received a call from the Hotel Perry, which was not all that surprising to him. After all, the seedy hotel, along with the nearby all-night restaurants, dive bars, and other rent-by-the-hour hotels in the three-block area, was well known to the Cleveland Police. What Detective Walker was concerned about, however, was that he was responding to a possible homicide based on the initial reports from his patrolmen already on scene.

On entering the dingy hotel room, it was hard not to gasp at the grisly scene in front of him. Even though Detective Walker had investigated many bloody homicides, including the gruesome hatchet murder of Dominick Mozela, king of the Black Hand Gang, it never really got easier, especially when it appeared that extreme violence was involved. And based on the condition of the young woman's body, Walker was certain that a vicious struggle had occurred.

Louis Bianchetti, charged with murdering Dolores Evans at the Hotel Perry in 1916. *From Acme Newspicture, Inc.*

Wearing only stockings, the victim lay half on and half off the bed. Bruises on her thighs, stomach, and breasts were immediately apparent. Leaning closer, the detective also noted spotty discoloration on her neck that resembled the impression of a thumb and fingerprint. Most shocking was the tatty hotel towel tied tightly around her head, covering her nose. Even with most of her face hidden, the detective could easily make out more purplish contusions on her face. Based on the condition of the body, it was clear that the woman had been dead for several hours.

Establishing that this was indeed a crime scene, the detective and his team further inspected the room, where they found a fake ruby ring, a cheap necklace, and a few nickels in the fingers of a pair of gloves. They also collected a cigar wrapper and women's clothing, most likely belonging to the deceased. They noted that the room was in minor disarray; the few pieces of furniture appeared to be out of place or shifted sideways.

Once the room was processed and the coroner called in, the next line of business was to determine who the victim was and who victimized her. The most obvious place to start was the front desk. Here Detective Walker learned the night maid, Ada Coffman, had shown the couple an available room around 11:45 p.m. After requesting a bucket of ice, the pair signed in as "Lou White and Wife" and headed for room 19 on the third floor.

With this new tidbit of information, Walker commissioned deputies to canvass the neighborhood to search for this Lou White character, as the detective had a few questions for the missing "husband."

In the meantime, Walker interviewed the proprietor, Jennie Smith, and night clerk, Sidney Blumenthal. While questioning the dynamic duo, it became apparent that the two were not so much concerned with helping solve the murder but more so in protecting the reputation of their fine establishment as well as its patrons. Although quite elaborate in their report on the events leading to the arrival of law enforcement, the two were rather vague in the details concerning their routine clientele. Most notably, for a place that was known to have guests checking in and out at all hours of the day, every room stood vacant at the time of Walker's appearance on scene, almost as though they had been warned ahead of time the police were on the way.

Despite Smith and Blumenthal's supposed ignorance, the clandestine activities at the Hotel Perry were no secret to the police. Like many other businesses in the area, the establishment was known to welcome prostitutes and their assortment of guests as well as other random couples that checked in for "immoral purposes," as reported numerous times in the *Cleveland Plain Dealer*. Several areas between East Ninth and East Twenty-Second Streets were considered a "zone of vice." These locations had popped up over the previous year as city officials and law enforcement had made a concentrated effort to shut down more widely known problem areas. Thus, Walker would be remiss to exclude the probability that his victim and her murderer were somehow caught up in Cleveland's underworld activities. Within a few hours of the investigation, this suspicion would prove to be correct.

Dolores Evans, who was found murdered in 1916. *From Acme Newspictures Inc.*

As Walker and his team continued to question staff at the hotel and employees of neighboring buildings, a couple arrived at the Hotel Perry inquiring about the identity of the deceased girl. George Pierce and Clara Dillie explained that they had been unable to locate their friend, Dolores Evans, since late the night prior. When Detective Walker described the victim and relayed the room number, Clara Dillie broke down into uncontrollable sobs as she became certain of her friend's fate.

According to Pierce and Dillie, they had been with Dolores when she met a man named Louis Bianchetti at the Chinese Republic restaurant. Soon after meeting, Dolores and the man took a cab across town to continue their date. Allegedly, Pierce and Dillie did not know where the pair was headed, but the two girls agreed to meet later that night back at the restaurant. In what seemed like an odd coincidence, Pierce and Dillie had later checked into the Hotel Perry and occupied the room directly below Dolores and Louis. When Dolores did not arrive at the agreed-on location later that morning, Dillie became concerned, so much so that when she learned of the discovery of a deceased woman at the hotel, she was filled with dread.

Now that he had some names to work with, the detective sent a couple of deputies out to search for Louis Bianchetti while he continued to acquire more information on the key players involved. Luckily, Clare Dillie had provided a recent photograph of Dolores Evans. One of the deputies recognized the woman as Elizabeth Myers, who had been arrested just a few months prior to the murder on charges of prostitution. Walker also learned that Dolores Evans rented a room at the Rexford Hotel, where she was asked to leave for "keeping ungodly hours." With this information, Walker was certain some type of illegal sexual activities had occurred in room 19.

Meanwhile, the deputies combed the neighborhood in search of Bianchetti. As evening descended on the streets and night shift employees returned to their post, the police were able to question those who may have worked or visited the surrounding businesses near the time of the murder. Working through the night and into the next morning, the team slowly traced the steps of Bianchetti back to the Roma Restaurant. There, they met Bianchetti's former boss, who provided a rough home address and mentioned Bianchetti's current place of employment at the Cleveland Athletic Club.

In the early afternoon the next day, Detective Walker and his men invaded the small apartment on East Eighteenth Street where Bianchetti had been living. Quickly they ascertained that the place had been swept clean of any trace of its inhabitant—that is, all traces had been removed except for an envelope that had been overlooked as someone made a hasty exit. Unfortunately for that someone, beautifully penned in the upper left corner of the envelope was a name and an address, which police found belonged to Bianchetti's sister in New York City. With this break in the case, Walker immediately dispatched a team to begin tracking their fugitive, who was now a day and a half ahead of them.

Unfortunately for Bianchetti, it was reported later that he did not appear to be that concerned with his predicament during the first day of the investigation. Perhaps he felt that the death of a prostitute at a dingy hotel would go unnoticed and uninvestigated. Or maybe he believed that it was unlikely that the crime could be traced back to such a fine upstanding fellow as himself. Possibly, as he would later claim, he believed that had not actually killed the woman but only knocked her out. Whatever his initial thoughts were, his immediate actions did not do him any favors in the eyes of the public when later it was suggested that he was a cold and unremorseful killer.

Before investigators arrived at the hotel, Bianchetti had made his way back to his apartment in the wee hours of the night. Here he grabbed a few hours of sleep to be fresh for his early shift at the club. On Wednesday morning, he clocked in for his duties and began his tasks of preparing culinary delights for the busy lunch rush. If anything was amiss, Bianchetti gave no indication, although one coworker noticed that the usually physically flawless Louis had vibrant red scratches on one of his cheeks. When asked, Bianchetti stated that a girl had tried to rob him while on a date.

Cleveland Athletic Club, where suspected murderer Louis Bianchetti worked as a chef. *Author's collection.*

By Thursday morning, as Bianchetti clocked in for another shift, it is possible that he believed that the whole event involving Dolores Evans was behind him. After all, there were no reports of it in the newspapers and no policemen had come banging down his door. It was probably as he had originally suspected and there would not be an investigation. Yet by midmorning, the employee chitchat had shattered this illusion: He overheard tale of a murdered woman on Prospect Avenue. Not only was the kitchen abuzz with talk of a vicious homicide not far from the club, but the press was also proudly proclaiming that the city had a "sadistic" killer, like Jack the Ripper, on the loose.

Here Bianchetti had his first jolt of panic, and he realized that the police were only steps behind him. The byline "Law's Net Circles Girl's Slayer" in the *Cleveland Plain Dealer* suggested as much. Sure, he used a fake name over there at that dump of a hotel, but that did not mean that they would not have a description of him based on his numerous interactions that evening. And according to the article, the dead girl's friend had provided a full description and possible address for her friend's killer. With this, Bianchetti knew he had to act fast.

Around ten o'clock on Thursday morning, Bianchetti approached his boss, the head chef, stating that he was in a bit of trouble and that he was quitting his position. He then demanded his back wages and hightailed it back to his apartment, where he promptly packed up his belongings. With one final sweep of the room, he hurriedly exited the premises, all the while keeping an eye out for any police officers who might be sniffing around. Not spotting anyone resembling law enforcement, Bianchetti hailed a cab and began his journey away from the city.

Soon after, Bianchetti arrived at Willow Station, located just south of Cleveland. Here, he bought a ticket to Akron. According to later witness testimony, Bianchetti gave no hint of being someone on the run. Instead, while awaiting the train, he was seen casually eating a sandwich and shooting a few rounds of pool in the adjacent café. A day later, the owner of the Willow Station Inn identified his customer as Louis Bianchetti based on a photo presented to him by the Cleveland Police.

When Bianchetti reached Akron, he disembarked at the Howard-Market Station and made his way to the popular Portage Hotel, where he inquired about a potential cook's position. Learning that no openings existed, he returned to the train station and proceeded to buy a ticket to Chicago. Here, the only flicker of anything unusual was that he bought a ticket to go west toward Chicago but boarded an eastbound train at the last minute according to the train station employees. Consequently, wires were sent to westbound stations to be on the lookout for a man matching Bianchetti's description. At the same, a message was dispatched to New York, on the assumption that the suspect was heading that way.

Regardless of Bianchetti's attempt to throw the law off his trail, his eventual arrest was swift. After arriving in New York City on Sunday afternoon, he made his way to Thirty-Fifth Street to the apartment of Olympia Caroli, his sister. What he did not realize was that the New York police had been staking out the apartment after receiving a call from Cleveland. Once they were certain they had the right man, the two detectives approached the residence and asked to speak to Bianchetti. After two hours of interrogation, Bianchetti confessed to the crime. His confession and subsequent arrest seemed to be going quite smoothly until the detectives located clothing and accessories belonging to the victim within the confessed killer's steamer trunk, which he had brought with him. This finding seemed to panic Bianchetti; he grabbed for a knife and threatened to kill himself if they took him back to Cleveland. Before he could do so, detectives were able to secure the knife and restrain him before taking him to the city jail.

Meanwhile, back in Cleveland, a morbid fascination with the deceased was emerging. Because there was confusion concerning the victim's identity, the officials allotted the public the chance to view the body in hopes that someone could make a definite identification and perhaps a proper burial could take place. What officials in the case were not expecting was that thousands of people, including the city's upper class, would make a day of it, arriving in their Sunday best with their children in tow. According to the *Cleveland Plain Dealer*, "That marble slab apparently proved as fascinating attraction for the hordes of curiosity seekers as a bargain sale or that of some other form of entertainment.... Little Dolores dead apparently commanded no more respect than little Dolores living."

While most of the morgue visitors were there to satisfy their curiosity, a few people held legitimate claims that they could identify the deceased. Although several names and identities were presented, including Minnie Roscoe of Garrettsville, Ohio, and Bernice Harris of Ontario, Canada, the name Myers and the city of Pittsburgh seemed to be most promising. First, a woman from Pennsylvania then living in Cleveland stated that she immediately recognized the girl as Elizabeth Myers of Becks Run, a suburb of Pittsburgh. Her claims were backed by Reverend Stoppel of Becks Run, who stated that the girl had come to him a couple of years earlier in search of her baptismal certificate, which she needed in order to marry. Another woman from Pittsburgh insisted that "Dolores Evans" was Elizabeth Schaubhut Myers, who had married her brother, a sailor with the U.S. Navy, but had since disappeared. Next, a man from Mansfield, Ohio, appeared at the morgue ready to claim the body of his niece Mary Myers. According to Wilson Truman, Mary came to live with him and his wife after her parents divorced. The girl had arrived from Pittsburgh when she was just fifteen and stayed with the Trumans for the next two years. Recently, she had told her uncle that she was returning to Pittsburgh, but the Trumans had not received information as to whether she made it. Lastly, police had arrested a girl by the name of Elizabeth Myers a couple months prior to the murder, a girl who looked exactly like the now deceased Dolores Evans.

Unfortunately, officials could not establish the victim's identity, so she was to be buried as Dolores Evans, the name she had given in recent months to her friends and acquaintances. Although she may not have been buried under her given name, her friends insisted that she would at least have a decent resting place instead of being interred in the potter's field, a space reserved for the unidentified, poor, and sometimes undesirable of the city. Instead, they pooled their funds together and bought a plot for her in Woodlawn Cemetery, where she eventually was laid to rest after being held in the cemetery's receiving vault for two weeks in the hopes that someone could officially identify her.

If the media was delighted to report on the crowds that came out to see the body, they were even more thrilled to report on the throngs of people awaiting Bianchetti's return to the city after his indictment in New York City. On Saturday, January 18, thousands crowded into Union Station, excitedly awaiting the train carrying its dark passenger. Spectators who were not lucky enough to score a spot within the station were not deterred. They simply lined up along Public Square near the courthouse, which also housed the jail. Either location had its pros, really. The station offered the first glimpse of the heartless monster while the street setting allowed for views of the murderer on his way to pay for his crime. Both permitted a chance for sneers and jeers as Bianchetti was paraded to the jail to await his arraignment.

From the get-go, prosecutor Cyrus Locher stated that the prosecution would go after a first-degree murder charge, which included the death penalty. With this, prosecution would need to prove premeditation. On the defense, attorney Sullivan planned to show that his client was tricked into a con job by Dolores and her accomplices and his actions that night were in reaction to a robbery, making him the victim. He had not intended to kill Dolores, but he had acted in defense. With a trial set for February 23, both sides had just a couple of weeks to prepare their arguments.

At the trial, the murder and the events leading up to the murder were pieced together via both Bianchetti and witness testimony. According to Bianchetti, he and Dolores Evans went to the Hotel Perry to have sexual relations that he would pay her for after the fact. Once the deed was done, he stated that he dozed off for a bit. When he awoke, he found Evans going through his coat pocket. When she realized that he was awake, she proceeded to throw his wallet out the window, which led Bianchetti to the realization that she was attempting to rob him. The now angered Bianchetti immediately sprang into action, and a physical altercation between the two ensued. During the incident, he struck the victim three to four times in the face, the final blow causing her to lose consciousness. At this point, he assumed she was still alive and tied a towel around her face and neck to keep her from screaming once she woke up. Quickly gathering his belongings, he fled the room but stopped under the window to look for his wallet, which he could not find. When he noticed footprints in the newly fallen snow that seemed to stop under the window, he was certain that he had been involved in a scam set up by Dolores and her friends.

Prosecutor Locher attempted to show that Bianchetti did not have money on his person that night. Instead, the accused was down on his luck and had asked to borrow five dollars from his friend on the night of Dolores's death. Not only that, but according to the testimonies of Clara Dillie and George Pierce, there never was and never had been robberies planned between the three friends. The murder then could only have been a result of madman who intentionally planned and even enjoyed the violent events that unfolded at the Hotel Perry.

As for the defense team, Sullivan based his argument on character witnesses for Bianchetti. He called many coworkers and acquaintances to the stand who insisted that the defendant was a good-natured fellow and hardworking young man. Attempting to prove that Bianchetti was a target that night, Sullivan called eyewitnesses from the chop suey restaurant who had seen his client flashing around a fat stack of cash. Thus, anyone, including Evans, Dillie, and Pierce, in the eatery looking for a mark would have seen the money as well. The sole purpose of the encounter between Evans and Bianchetti was set up by Pierce. The trio clearly planned to rob his client and go about their night, but the job did not go according to plan. Instead, Bianchetti fought back and unintentionally killed Evans in defense of his property.

After seven days of trial, Bianchetti's fate rested in the hands of the judge and jury. Because the prosecution could not prove premeditation, the first-degree murder charge was off the table. After eight hours of deliberation, the jury returned with a guilty verdict of manslaughter. The judge, also showing mercy, sentenced Bianchetti to the Ohio Penitentiary to serve a sentence of one to twenty years with the possibility of parole after one year.

In 1919, with four years of demonstrated model behavior at the London Prison Farm, where he was eventually transferred and often worked in the kitchen as a cook, he was released.

For Louis Bianchetti, a night on the town resulted in shouldering the shame of the city's underworld and a four-year stint in prison. After his release, he seemingly disappeared, perhaps changing his name and moving as far from Cleveland as possible. As for Dolores Evans, an evening working the streets to earn a living ended in the most horrific way possible, illuminating the desperate life of many young women like her. Most likely from the shame involved, her real family never claimed her, or it is possible they never knew of her fate. For both, their young lives were shattered by a deadly game that they played behind closed doors.

THE SECRET
(TOLEDO, 1935)

Seventeen-year-old Dorothy Brown had a secret. Although she knew little about the subject, she knew enough to understand that her life was about to change. After missing two menstrual cycles and now with the nausea setting in, especially in the mornings, it was time to reveal her secret to the one person who would know what to do.

Winnona Brown had been aware that her daughter had grown somewhat withdrawn during the fall of 1935. She had attributed it to the girl's busy schedule as a high school senior who was involved in many academic and civic clubs. After all, attending Scott High, one of Toledo's largest schools, offered students many extracurriculars on top of an expectation for excellence in scholarly achievements. Perhaps it was a lot of pressure on Dorothy, who always sought to be a good daughter and student. Thus, when Dorothy asked if she could speak to Winnona in private in early December, she wondered if the girl would disclose that she was struggling to keep up with her schoolwork, chores, and assortment of clubs and organizations. A few hours later, after she made sense of what her daughter had explained between sobs, Winnona wished that unfinished homework was the issue at hand.

Once the pregnancy was confirmed via a discreet visit to the doctor's office, and George, Dorothy's father, settled down from his initial shock, the next step was for Dorothy to speak to the father of her unborn child. Oddly, Dorothy did not have a steady boyfriend—or at least one that either parent had met. Strangely, as far as her family knew, Dorothy had

A romantic-themed postcard popular in the early 1900s. *Author's collection.*

only casually dated over the last couple of years and did not seem to be in a hurry for a serious relationship. So, when Dorothy announced that a man by the name of Bob Robinson was the father, it was the first time her parents had heard of him.

According to Dorothy, the relationship, if it could be called that, began in late August, when twenty-four-year-old Bob Robinson, who worked at the Toledo Scale Company near the high school, offered to give Dorothy a ride home. Over the next few weeks, the rides continued, and the conversation grew a little more flirtatious with each new encounter. Like most girls, Dorothy was flattered by the attention of an older man, especially one who had a job and could drive. Eventually, the two took their conversations to more private locations, which included secluded back roads and parking spots along the Ohio-Michigan border. By early October, the pair were crossing more than just the state line as their dates turned physically intimate.

Sometime in November, Dorothy began to suspect that she may be pregnant. When she was almost certain of it, she then decided to tell her mother. With this information, and the pregnancy confirmed, Winnona insisted that Dorothy must tell her boyfriend. After all, he should take some responsibility for his own child. Obeying her mother, and perhaps hoping that Bob would offer to marry her, Dorothy arranged to go for a drive with him.

On December 15, parked along a darkened Petersburg Road, south of Sylvania, Michigan, Dorothy revealed her secret to Bob. Although she had not expected him to be overjoyed, she was not prepared for his response. Immediately, he angrily claimed that he was not the father and that Dorothy must have been with another man. The more she argued that he was the father and would be partially responsible for the baby, the more furious Bob became, practically spitting at her as he denied his paternity. Although she had never seen this side of her lover, she had no inclination that she should be scared. Even as he began frantically digging around under the driver's seat, Dorothy made no attempt to stop him, nor did she try to protect herself as he swung the object above her head.

Meanwhile, Winnona, aware of the date and the planned conversation between her daughter and Bob, had harbored a bad feeling from the moment that Dorothy got into that man's car. As she watched the two drive away earlier that evening, a heavy sensation descended on the concerned mother, prompting her to commit the license plate number to memory. Certainly, she had coaxed Dorothy to speak with Bob, but now as the hours

Scott High School in Toledo, where Dorothy Brown was a senior. *Author's collection.*

passed by, she wondered if it had been a good idea to let the girl go alone. Consequently, by the next morning, after Dorothy failed to appear without explanation, Winnona's nervousness had built into a full-blown panic. By the time the police car rolled into the driveway several hours later, Winnona braced herself for the worst as George opened the door.

According to Detective Owen Green and Ray Sheets, Dorothy had been admitted to Flower Hospital of Toledo after she was found unconscious in a ditch along Petersburg Road in Michigan, about ten miles from the Browns' home, on the morning of December 16. Hospital staff reported that she had a massive head injury that appeared to be inflicted by blunt-force trauma. Along with a severe skull fracture, the young woman had been exposed to frigid temperatures for an elongated period and was in critical condition. Both doctors and police concluded that Dorothy was the victim of a violent crime, and the detectives were at the Browns' home to not only alert the parents of their daughter's state but also to open a full investigation.

As Winnona digested the news of the brutal attack, Detective Sheets questioned both her and George about the last time they had seen their daughter. With this, an image of Dorothy hopping into that car the night before filled Winnona's mind. Immediately, she filled in the detective on the details of the date and the life-altering news that Dorothy planned to deliver. When pressed for more details, Winnona was able to provide the license plate number, explaining that she felt uneasy once the date was in motion and had memorized the number.

Using this information provided by Winnona, Detective Green set to tracking down Bob for questioning. However, when he traced the plate number, he found that that the vehicle was registered to a man named John Kurtz, age twenty-four, of Toledo, whom he immediately hauled in for questioning.

During the interview, they informed Kurtz that Michigan State Police had found Dorothy Brown barely alive, thrown into a ditch alongside the road. Surprisingly, without much prompting at all, Kurtz confessed to the crime, although he did insinuate that Dorothy had provoked him by demanding $500 for a child that most likely was not his. He explained how they had argued, with Dorothy threatening to call the police. Finally, he stated, "By this time, I was so angry that I saw black. Then I hit her….I can't believe that I was so cruel," as reported in the *Detroit Press Extra*.

Digging further into Kurtz's background, the detectives were able to piece together a possible motive for the attack. Apparently, John Kurtz was a married man with a wife and a nine-month-old son at home. Originally from Blissfield, Michigan, Kurtz had secured work at the Toledo Scale Company a few years prior. Married in 1934, he and his wife, May, settled in Toledo to be closer to his job. In early 1935, a few months before his encounters with Dorothy, the couple had welcomed a son, Bobbie. His pseudonym illustrated Kurtz's dishonest nature and his attempt to keep the affair with Dorothy a secret.

As the press picked up on the story, referring to it as another *American Tragedy* case, more details emerged, especially concerning Kurtz. Reporters learned that John Kurtz had been a star athlete in both football and basketball at Blissfield High School. Along with his athleticism, he held down a job at a local bakery, working the 4:00 a.m. shift before school. Graduating in 1929, Kurtz began work at the Toledo company, where he quickly moved up the ladder from delivery truck driver to working in the business planning department, the youngest person to do so within the company. Although they could not find any criminal blemish in Kurtz's past, a few intriguing personal tidbits were deemed newsworthy.

According to reports, John Kurtz was married to his former English high school teacher, May Warner, who was six years his elder. Although it is uncertain when the relationship began, the two had been openly dating since 1932, three years after his graduation. By all accounts, including

May's later testimony, the marriage had been a happy one as she was content to stay at home with little Bobbie while John worked to further build a successful career. Recently, the couple had learned that they were expecting a second child, as May was nearly three months pregnant at the time of John's arrest.

Dorothy Brown, found beaten in a ditch near Toledo, 1935. *From Acme Newspictures Inc.*

While the press continued to dig, Kurtz waived extradition rights and was sent to the Monroe County Jail in Michigan, where he would await his arraignment pending Dorothy's recovery. If she succumbed to her injuries, Kurtz would be charged with murder. If she survived, he would be charged with assault with a dangerous weapon. On Friday, December 20, three days after the attack, Dorothy's doctors reported that she was showing signs of improvement. Thus, Kurtz was arraigned the same day, pleading not guilty to the charge of assault with intention to do great bodily harm. His bail was set at $5,000 and a court date set for early February 1936

In the interim, the media's focus was on the relationships between John Kurtz, his wife, and his young lover. Since the press did not have access to Dorothy and Kurtz remained tight-lipped due to his impending trial, the spotlight turned once again to May Kurtz, who was willing to talk as a means of defending her husband. May reiterated that John was a great husband and she planned to stand by him throughout the ordeal. She also shouldered some of the blame concerning the affair, suggesting that she had been consumed with childcare and not as attentive as she should have been to her husband, who had been staying out late at night since the baby's arrival. Regardless of his mistakes, May stood firm on her resolve, stating that she would support John, as "he's been a fine husband and father," as reported in the *Detroit Press*.

On February 24 began John Kurtz's trial for assault with intent to kill, which carried a life sentence if found guilty. During his testimony, he did not deny the affair with Dorothy but insisted that she encouraged him, basically throwing herself at him. He also stated that Dorothy said the father could be John or possibly another man by the name of Ted. As a result of her promiscuousness, when she demanded payment, he refused, as he was unsure of the paternity of the child. When Dorothy threatened to call the police on him, that is when he reacted, claiming that "everything went black" and he did not remember hitting her with the wrench or dumping her out of the vehicle. Additionally, his defense called several character witnesses to the stand, including his foreman at the Toledo Scale Company and his pastor. May and John's father, Edward, attended the trial and continued to show support for John throughout the case.

On the other side, the prosecution called Dorothy, who had made a full recovery, to the stand as their star witness. She shared how she had met John Kurtz, known then as Bob Robinson, while walking home, when he offered to give her a ride home. He made no mention of being married or having a child. The relationship continued via a series of clandestine rides along the back roads over the fall of 1935. In early December, she realized that she was with child and planned to tell John, whom she claimed was the only man she had been with in her young life. She described the conversation that took place on December 15 on Petersburg Road and how John quickly became angry, completely denying his part in the pregnancy. She recalled that he fumbled around with something under the seat but did not remember being hit over the head or lying in the ditch for nearly thirteen hours.

On February 27, after an hour and twenty-three minutes of deliberation, the jury returned the verdict of guilty of felonious assault, which carried a far lesser penalty than the charge of assault with intent to kill. Circuit Judge Clayton C. Goldman sentenced Kurtz to a term of three years and nine months to four years imprisonment to be served in the Ionia Reformatory in Ionia, Michigan. Clearly frustrated that the jury took pity on Kurtz, Judge Goldman stated, "You are very a lucky man. I would have no hesitancy in finding you guilty of the major crime in which you were charged."

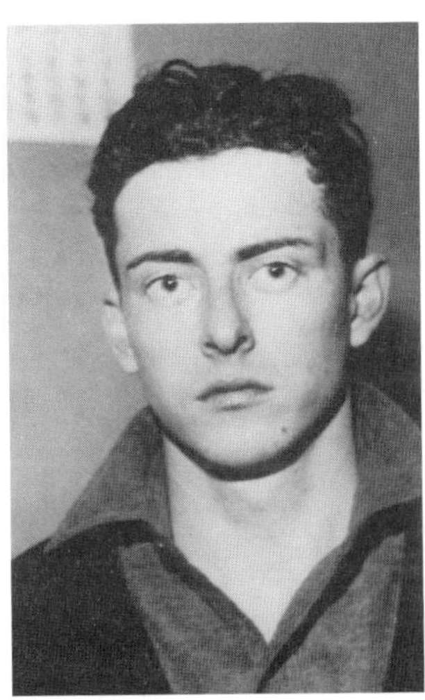
John Kurtz, charged with attacking Dorothy Brown, his former lover, 1935. *From Acme Newspictures Inc.*

As John Kurtz served his time, the theme of tragedy persisted within the Kurtz family. In June 1937, a year and a half after John was sentenced, his father, Edward, hanged himself in his Blissfield home. In 1940, May Kurtz, still married to John, died of sickness, leaving Bobbie and Gloria, John's second child, to her sister to raise. Bobbie went on to become a star athlete in high school. On his graduation, he joined the U.S. Army and became a major, but he was killed in Vietnam when his helicopter was shot down in 1967. The high school where he graduated still awards the Robert Warner Kurtz Scholarship each year.

John Kurtz was released on parole in June 1939. According to the 1950 census, he had remarried. He died in 1980.

As for Dorothy Brown, she gave birth to a baby boy in 1916, whom her parents helped raise. Later, she married in 1955 and moved to Washington State. It is unclear whether she had additional children.

THE BEWITCHING OF SAMUEL AND MATILDA WALDMAN (CLEVELAND, 1935)

Witchcraft is not dead in America, nor did the last of witches burn during the days of the Salam witchcraft.
—Lancaster Examiner, 1904

After asking nicely to have the hex removed, Matilda Waldman realized that she had only one other option when it came to ending the curse that had plagued both herself and her husband for several years. From suspicious health issues and near financial ruin to most recently the literal fireballs that shot through their apartment every night, the misery inflicted on them was more than they could bear. Thus, on a humid August morning in 1935, Matilda decided she would have to send the evil back to the darkness from where it came.

During their interrogation at Central Station—after the evil had been eradicated—fifty-two-year-old Samuel and forty-year-old Matilda Waldman told Cleveland detectives that the trouble started over twenty years prior to the day of reckoning. In 1912, Samuel met a woman by the name of Ida Rose Cooper in Pittsburgh, where he was living at the time. During their short friendship, Ida convinced a reluctant Samuel to attend a seminar on black magic. At the meeting held on Federal Street on the second floor of a darkened building, women were instructed in the art of creating fireballs and then shown how to direct the burning fist-sized orbs in specific paths of motion. By the end of training, several of the women, including Ida Cooper, had perfected the skill.

A romantic-themed postcard popular in the early 1900s. *Author's collection.*

Fearing what he considered to be the devil's work, Samuel refused to attend another meeting and distanced himself from Ida Cooper. Months later, however, Samuel began to suffer odd symptoms, including rashes, bruises, and cuts. Likewise, Samuel's first wife and five children started to complain of similar problems, which doctors could not explain. When fist-sized fireballs began shooting through their home late at night, Samuel connected the dots or, in this case, balls of fire. He was convinced that he had been hexed. For what reasons, he was unsure, but he was certain that the sorcerer was none other than Ida Cooper.

Over the next several years, Samuel and his wife suffered under the malicious spell until they could take it no more. In 1918, in an attempt to escape the curse, the family moved from Pittsburgh to Detroit. Meanwhile, Ida and her husband, Isadore Cooper, relocated to Cleveland.

With the hope that they were free of Ida and her voodoo, Samuel concentrated on starting a new life with his wife and children in the then thriving city of Detroit. Striking out on an optimistic note, Samuel tried his hand as an entrepreneur and opened his own restaurant. Immediately, Samuel noticed unexplainable issues occurring within his business. From high-dollar financial mistakes to a freezer with a month's worth of food that mysteriously rotted away, the dream of owning a restaurant turned into a nightmare of frequent customer complaints and eventual bankruptcy.

If losing the business was not bad enough, Samuel and his family were again plagued with recurring health issues. Month after month, the family experienced everything from severe flu-like symptoms to painful rashes and sores. Additionally, amid their physical anguish, the flying fireballs began to appear once again. Realizing that the spell was still on them, Samuel's wife took the children and fled from Detroit in the company of another man, leaving Samuel alone, penniless, and cursed.

Over the next few years, Samuel eked out a meager living selling men's razors and lightbulbs, all the while continuing to suffer under the hex. Believing that he was destined to a life of misery, he was pleasantly surprised in 1931 when he met Matilda, who seemed quite receptive to his company. Although she was fourteen years his junior, Matilda seemed not to mind the age difference, and a romance between the two quickly blossomed. Samuel, taking no risks of losing his second chance at love, did not disclose to Matilda that he came with baggage in the form of a curse and hid his numerous illnesses from her. Fortunately for Samuel, Matilda never became suspicious and instead agreed to marry him just a few months into the relationship. Nevertheless, even with Samuel's extra precautions in place, it was not long before his secret reared its ugly head.

Matilda Waldman, also known as the Hex Killer, charged with murdering Ida Cooper, 1935. *Courtesy of Cleveland Public Library Photograph Collection.*

As the couple began their life together, Samuel suffered intense pain and unrelenting illness, which he could barely hide from Matilda. When Matilda started to complain of strange sores on her legs and debilitating fatigue and depression, Samuel had no other choice but to tell his new bride that not only was he cursed, but apparently Matilda was as well. Unconvinced, Matilda insisted that the two see a doctor who could diagnose their ailments using medical science. Instead, as both Matilda and Samuel later explained, the doctor immediately recognized the telltale signs of voodoo magic and sent them away without a remedy or cure.

Now frightened, especially once the fireballs appeared in the night, Matilda suggested that the couple attempt to flee farther from the source of evil, which they knew resided in Cleveland only a few hours from their home in Detroit. Leaving in the middle of the night, they made their way to California. Believing that the distance and possibly the beauty of their new environment would end or at least alleviate the effects of the curse, they looked forward to starting a new life on the West Coast. Yet before they could fully settle down, the couple began to experience pinprick sensations all over their bodies. Frustratingly, they realized that it was only a matter of time before the more severe symptoms would occur. On top of this, Samuel struggled to hold down a job, which he attributed as another effect of the blasted evil spell.

By June 1935, after suffering almost four years together, Samuel and Matilda had finally had enough. Together, they decided that the only way to end this was to face the source head-on. Packing their belongings, they headed east but not to Michigan. Instead, they arrived in Cleveland, where they began a search for Ida Cooper, whom they planned to confront and demand that she stop this nonsense once and for all. After all, Samuel had lived under her spell for over two decades and he had paid greatly for whatever injustice that Ida had perceived worthy of her wicked magic.

Before long, and after locating Ida and Isadore Cooper, the Waldmans secured an apartment on 105th Street West, located about one mile from the Coopers' home and about six blocks from their delicatessen shop. Unfortunately, before they had a chance to speak to the Coopers, the symptoms of the curse resumed, seemingly with more intensity. During the first night at their new residence, the fireballs shot through their bedroom faster and more numerous than ever before. On waking up the next morning, Samuel was violently ill. It was as though the witch had been waiting for them and was now unleashing her full power.

The Waldmans' first attempt at asking fifty-two-year-old Ida to end the curse was to no avail. Entering the Coopers' deli, the Waldmans approached Ida, who was busy behind the counter. Instantly, Ida recognized Samuel from their time in Pittsburgh. Assuming the visit was a social call, Ida was perplexed when Matilda demanded that she end the curse that she had cast on Samuel all those years ago. Hearing this, Ida dismissed the accusations as a misunderstanding. Even though she did dabble in the occult sciences and often read neighbors' palms or predicted their futures through her crystal ball, she had never hexed another person. The entire notion was ridiculous, and she dismissed the Waldmans with a chuckle and nod toward the exit.

To Samuel and Matilda, Ida's reaction only illustrated her cold and evil heart. Here they were, after years living in torture, kindly asking her to end it, and she basically laughed in their faces. In fact, it seemed to the Waldmans that Ida only ramped up the force of her hatred when, just days after the encounter, Samuel became partially blind in one eye and began to experience intermittent paralysis throughout the following weeks.

In a continued effort to stop the madness, the Waldmans, especially Samuel, made daily visits to the Coopers' home and deli, demanding that Ida lift the spell. In response to Samuel's appearance at their properties, sometimes more than once a day, the Coopers became increasingly annoyed, pleading with him to stop his hounding. At one point, Isadore and Ida went to the Waldmans' apartment and requested that they stop their harassment. This visit resulted in a heated argument without either side procuring any relief from their perceived tormentors.

Over the following days, the Waldmans continued to fight off the attacks associated with the hex. First, they covered all the mirrors and windows in their home, as they believed this would somehow stop the evil that powered the fireballs. When this did not work, they barricaded every crack and crevice in the home, including the keyholes, so that the orbs could not enter. Soon, though, they realized they were helpless against the supernatural objects and resorted to taking turns keeping watch over their home throughout the night. During the watch, they would swat at the orbs with a hammer, which sometimes destroyed the fiery balls by exploding them into small pieces of ash. Other times they would attempt to nail the projectiles to the wall or to an anvil. During the day, they attempted to fight the black magic by lighting a fire and holding their faces close to it. No matter what tactic they tried, though, the curse continued gaining strength, while the Waldmans' fixation with ending it grew out of control.

Late in July, Matilda attempted yet another strategy with Ida. Entering the deli, Matilda produced a handwritten note in which she demanded that Ida sign an agreement. The message read, "I Ida Rose or Ida Cooper agree to release Mr. & Mrs. Waldman and his children and family from the witch craft I have done till now and I will never do witch craft to the Waldman family any more all my life."

On reading this, Ida refused to sign and instead expressed her annoyance with Matilda and her constant pestering. She once again explained that she had never hexed anyone and did not possess the power to do so. Realizing that Ida would not lift the curse, let alone acknowledge it, Matilda stormed out of the deli with the unsigned contract in hand.

I:- Ida Rose, or Ida Cooper
agree to release Mr Mrs
Waldman + his children
and family from the
witch craft. I have
done till now + I will
never do witch craft
to Waldman family any
more all my life

The handwritten contract that the Waldmans wanted Ida Cooper to sign to end the supposed curse. *Courtesy of Cleveland Public Library Photograph Collection.*

As the summer wore on, so too did the relentless agony that plagued the Waldmans, which was only exacerbated by several heat waves in late July and early August. To make matters worse, they kept their windows and doors stuffed with paper and rags, blocking any fireballs as well as ventilation in an already stifling hot apartment. As their physical misery worsened, their obsession with Ida Cooper and her diabolical methods became more pronounced. Consequently, neighbors took note of the bizarre behavior and watched as the peculiar couple descended deeper into their madness, often hearing loud chanting for hours at a time coming from within the barricaded residence.

Meanwhile, between chanting sessions and hammering fireballs to the walls, Samuel continued to bombard the Coopers, loitering in front of their home and barging into their deli. Still, the Coopers refused to remove the curse and continued to deny that Ida was ever a practicing witch. After a particularly hostile visit to the deli on a blistering hot July 31, Samuel came to the realization that his attempts were futile and that it was time to seek outside help. Feeling completely defeated, Samuel headed toward Cleveland's Central Station to report his tormentor.

On that same day, Isadore Cooper decided that he too could take no more. Unbeknownst to Samuel, Isadore arrived at the station minutes behind him. While Samuel reported Ida's refusal to remove the curse and her relentless torture via the spell, Isadore recounted how the Waldmans had harassed his family for the past two months. Sorting out the fiasco, assistant prosecutor William Schneider deemed that Waldman should stop pestering the Coopers. He also advised Cooper that if Waldman persisted, he should petition a warrant of insanity for Samuel. As the men left the station, both feeling that their complaints were still unresolved, they had no idea that that they would return the next day with a much bigger and deadlier problem.

Later that afternoon, Matilda seethed within the barricaded apartment. For her, the conclusion of the police visit was the last straw. After all the begging and pleading and especially after all the suffering at the hands of Ida Cooper, her poor Samuel, now in grave health, had no other choice but to trek all the way downtown to speak with the police, who acted as though the Waldmans were the troublemakers. With this latest development, Matilda simmered with what she realized was hatred for Ida. In those moments, it became clear to her that the witch had to be stopped one way or another, even if it came to a physical altercation.

The following day, August 1, after Samuel left for work, Matilda quickly dressed. Slamming out of her apartment door, she began the march toward the Coopers' deli, where she knew Ida would be working. As she stormed down the familiar path, she hesitated for just a moment. Yet her pause was not due to indecision. Instead, as Matilda would explain to the police later, she began to hear a voice telling her that she should return home to retrieve a gun for her own protection. After all, Ida was capable of violence, as she had shown repeatedly.

On entering the deli, with her revolver hidden in her handbag, Matilda approached Ida, who was stocking the shelves. As Ida turned to greet her potential customer, she threw her hands up in exasperation when she recognized Matilda. Noting the negative nonverbal greeting, Matilda angrily launched into her speech, basically demanding that Ida lift the curse as well as sign the contract Matilda had presented weeks prior. Infuriatingly to Matilda, her demands were met in the same manner as before, with Ida denying the witchery and refusing to sign the agreement. To add to the already tension-fused situation, according to Matilda, Ida "put her hands in the air and then pulled her hair down over her eyes and began to bewitch again" by running through the store and casting her spells, as reported in the *Pittsburgh Sun-Telegraph*.

As Ida recited her incantations, Matilda heard the voice once again, this time telling her to retrieve the gun from her purse. Between Ida's chaotic dance with the devil and the voice that whispered in her air, Matilda frantically whipped the gun from its hiding place and took aim. The first bullet hit Ida in the arm, freezing her in the midst of her satanic ritual. The next bullet zipped through her left breast while a third bullet whizzed by her head without hitting her. Pausing to survey the damage, Matilda watched as Ida fell to the floor and ceased to move. Later, it would be determined that Ida most likely died within minutes, as the second bullet had pierced her heart.

Satisfied that the deed was done, Matilda turned and ran from the store. Noting that a crowd had already gathered outside after hearing the commotion from within, Matilda yelled out that there had been a holdup and a man had shot the female owner of the deli. The man, according to the distraught Matilda, had fled from the store and the police should be called at once.

Arriving on scene, Sergeant Stephen Tozzer listened as Matilda explained what she had observed. However, other witnesses insisted that they had seen Matilda enter the store and exit minutes after the sounds of gunfire. They had not witnessed anyone else coming or going from the deli in the time in question. In fact, many of the witnesses reported that there had been ongoing verbal altercations between the Waldmans and Coopers for weeks leading up to the shooting.

Suspicious now of Matilda, Tozzer asked to search her handbag, where he located the .32-caliber revolver with three shells in the chamber. Realizing that she had been caught, Matilda began to tear up as she looked at the policeman and said, "Boy, please feel for me as it was my last resort. But I am relieved now. I was paralyzed by balls of fire. I could not see out of my eyes. I lost my speech. I couldn't eat or sleep while the spell was upon me." With a confession secured, Tozzer hauled the woman downtown.

During her ride to the station and later while being interrogated by a team of detectives, Matilda continued to describe the years of misery that both she and Samuel had suffered at the hands of the now deceased Ida. She explained how they had tried numerous strategies to end the curse, with each failing miserably. Her only resort, then, was to stop the evil at the source, which entailed killing Ida Cooper. With each detail met with looks of confusion on the policemen's faces, Matilda voiced her frustration several times by screaming, "She was a witch!"

Matilda Waldman behind bars as she awaits her trial for the murder of Ida Cooper, 1935. *Courtesy of Cleveland Public Library Photograph Collection.*

Meanwhile, Samuel was brought to the station and led past the room where Matilda was being booked. Cheerfully, he greeted his wife with a "Hello, honey," which was returned with a singsong "Hello, sweetheart," from Matilda. During his interview, Samuel exhibited the same happy demeanor as he explained that, while he had no knowledge of his wife's intentions to kill Ida, he was glad that she had done so. In fact, he stated that he felt immediate relief from the curse within the hour of the shooting. As Samuel rambled, echoing Matilda's proclamations of curses and fireballs, detectives began to question his sanity and sent him to the nearest hospital for a psychological evaluation.

The next day in municipal court, Matilda reiterated to Judge Joseph Ackerman that she was content with her actions. When the judge asked her if she meant that she was glad she had committed murder, Matilda patiently explained that it was not murder in her opinion. Instead, according to the accused, killing a witch was not the same as killing a human being. Additionally, she expressed that she felt more than satisfied with her decision. Moreover, she had not seen a single fireball the previous night and had slept like a baby. After listening to her ramblings, Judge Ackerman bound her over to the grand jury, without bail, on charges of first-degree murder.

On September 19, 1935, Matilda was indicted on a first-degree murder charge by the grand jury. The following day, she pleaded "not guilty by reason of insanity," for which Common Pleas Judge Alva Corlett appointed two doctors over the case to evaluate Matilda's mental health. After two months of interviewing family members, researching both Samuel and Matilda's background, and conferring with other expert psychologists, Dr. Royal G. Grossman and Dr. Louis Karnosh reported the following: "Matilda Waldman is suffering from a deeply entrenched paranoia. It has existed since she lived with her common-law husband, Samuel Waldman, who manifests a long-standing paranoid dementia....Prior to her marriage she had no paranoid ideas about witch craft....She believed everything he said, accepted all his rationalizations, became obsessed by the same delusions of which he formulated and very gradually convinced herself that life was intolerable as long as she and her husband were bewitched by one Ida Cooper."

The doctors went on to explain that Matilda's mental age and intellect were that of a thirteen-year-old. At the time of the murder and during recent evaluations, she exhibited no ability to choose right from wrong. They asserted that both Matilda and Sameul suffered from folie à deux, or "lunacy for two," in which one person's delusional beliefs are transmitted and eventually shared by another. On top of this, she would have been easily swayed by Samuel's convictions as she neared the age of menopause, which would make her more vulnerable to mental health issues, in their expert opinion. As a result of the medical findings, the judge ruled that Matilda be committed to the Lima State Hospital for the Criminally Insane.

A few months later, Samuel, who had undergone numerous psychological evaluations as well as in-depth interrogations concerning his part in the murder, was declared insane and sent to a sanitorium in Michigan. Both

Matilda Waldman at her release in 1939, after she was declared sane. *Courtesy of Cleveland Public Library Photograph Collection.*

his medical team as well as law officials deemed that he had no knowledge of his wife's plans to murder Ida, and even if he did, he would have met the same fate as Matilda: a life sentence to be served in a state mental hospital. Instead, Samuel spent several months at the sanitorium and was released into the care of his relatives in the spring of 1936. He passed away in or around the year 1950.

As for Matilda, she was released from the Lima State Hospital in 1939 after her sanity was found to be restored. A three-judge court acquitted Matilda of the murder of Ida Cooper, declaring that she committed the crime while she was clinically insane. Interestingly, she claimed that she had never been married to or lived with Samuel Waldman, and she planned to return to her parents' home in Detroit but refused to provide the family name to protect their privacy. When asked about her belief in witches, she stated, "I have heard of the presence of witches. You can be in a room with a lot of people, having a good time, and suddenly somebody will come in that casts a damper over everybody. You know that this person is possessed. The happiness will be gone."

BIBLIOGRAPHY

Newspapers

Akron Beacon Journal
American Weekly
Canton Daily News
Canton Repository
Carey Times
Cleveland Plain Dealer
The Daily News
Daily News Tribune
Dayton Daily News
Detroit Press
East Liverpool Evening Review
Evansville Courier and Press
Evening Review
Grand Rapids Press
Greenville Democrat
Lansing State Journal
Lima Morning Star and Republic Gazette
Lima Star
Mansfield News Journal
Marion Star
Newark Advocate
New York Times
Philadelphia Inquirer
Pittsburgh Press
Pittsburgh Sun-Telegraph
Salem News
Sandusky Register
Springfield News-Sun
Toledo Blade
Toledo News-Bee
Zanesville Signal

Magazines

Ben-Zeev, Aaron. "Why Do (Some) Men Murder the Wives They Love?" *Psychology Today*, 2014. https://www.psychologytoday.com.
Burkeholder, Edward. "Passions Proxy." *True Police Cases*, March 1951.
"Hear No Evil, Speak No Evil, See No Evil." *True Detective*, 1951.

Books

Anderson, Ann. *Snake Oil, Hustlers and Hambones*. McFarland, 2015.

Websites

Archives of Michigan. "Corrections Research." https://shop.michiganology.org.
Family Search. https://www.familysearch.org.
Find a Grave. https://www.findagrave.com.

Special Collections

M. Watt Espy Papers, 1730–2008. M.E. Grenander Department of Special Collections & Archives. https://archives.albany.edu.

ABOUT THE AUTHOR

Wendy Koile is a lifelong resident of Ohio who is fascinated with obscure Ohio and maritime history. She has authored four books focusing on lost tales of Ohio: *Geneva on the Lake: A Brief History of Ohio's First Resort*, *Legend and Lost Treasures of Ohio*, *Disasters of Ohio's Lake Erie Islands*, and *Lake Erie Murder and Mayhem*. She also shares maritime history as a guest lecturer on cruise ships. Wendy holds a master's degree in English as well as master's in teaching. When not writing or teaching, Wendy enjoys spending time with her family and pets.